THE CLASH

ROCK RETROSPECTIVES

by Ray Lowry
and Ben Myers

ANGRY PENGUIN
PUBLISHING LTD

Published by Angry Penguin Publishing Ltd
ISBN: 978-1-906283-36-0

2

THE CLASH

JOE AND MICK...

THE CLASH

I first witnessed the Clash down the bill on the infamous 'Anarchy' tour of Britain back in November of 1976 at the old, inglorious Electric Circus in Manchester.

Like most of the crowd (probably) I had gone along to witness the, by then, notorious SEX PISTOLS and I was largely unaware of Joe and the boys, saving the odd mention in the music press or Sniffin' Glue. They hit my unsuspecting nerve ends like a sharp jolt of high voltage electricity as soon as they appeared on the ratty old stage and I was immediately stripped of any extraneous mental baggage I had dragged along to that wild event. Sartorially and intellect--ually I was overdressed.

Joe and Mick made crazy dashes at the audience like a cultural battering ram determ--ined to smash down any faintheart prejudices or lazy preconceptions of what they were about. Only connect. A few songs into their set and ▶

I knew that this brand of
so-called PUNK ROCK was on
nodding aquaintance terms
with the mighty left field
mavericks and lunatics of my
nineteen fifties teenagedom
- teenagedumb, and the dying
gods of 'sixties rockdom.
But hold, these upstarts were
singing of things most familiar
and hearteningly apposite
to those benighted times of
the late nineteen seventies.
Only relate. Tower block
rat-trap living, garage
bands (?), being piss poor
and utterly insignificant.
Crappy jobs and no prospects
of anything better.
Living for the weekend and
whatever crappy drugs you
can get hold of (come in Eddie
Cochran, Gene Vincent and Charles
Berry). Faithless women
naturally, the old story right
back to Hank (vomits on stage
y'know) Williams. 
I felt a wholly familiar shiver
of recognition run down to the back of my
kneecaps as the Clash plugged into and

reshaped, remoddled and quite
amazingly redefined once more.
that bloody glorious song of old,
new and forever and ever, amen.
And women.
I confess that Johnny Thunders
and his boys and even the
Godalmighty S. Pistols were
shaded away into a sort
of also-ran position after
the unexpected ferocity
and total RELEVANCE
of these ill-attired,
paint spattered (long
before the Stoned Roses)
cockerny upstarts,
All thoughts of still trying
to squeeze some semblance
of authenticity out of "DESPERADO" era
Eagles albums (people did, I was there,
reader) and the likes of the Ozark Mountain
Daredevils had been dashed by the likes of
the Ramones and reissues of MC5 and
Igpop albums; but here was the new real
deal, fresh out of Camden and singing wiv
a Nenglish accent, God help us.
for a taste of this early ferocity I can only
point you to the Munich footage featured in
the extras to the RUDE BOY DVD..

SUBURBIA ROCKED!i

The months of waiting until May of '77 and the release of 'The Clash' are still entirely memorable. Could the band really reproduce that mad stage shit on vinyl? Like all the real talents from Elvis down to the Beatles they could and, by golly, they did. I played that tinny, (to those with tin ears) under--produced wunderdisc for hours on end just as I had last done with the first Rolling Stones outing on a hot summer night a decade and more earlier. The Clash album (and the Rolling Stones similar) didn't pall and never has.
I saw the chaps intermittently through the years that followed striking up a nodding, ▶

conversing kind of on-off relationship with the
chaps. Nothing was ever formal
with the Clash unless you
wanted to throw your lot in
completely and join the team.
Some tried and failed, witness
the abject Ray Gange in
Rude Boy. As a
committed
outsider   to
every-   -thing
          that looked
          like a cause
      and/or hard work
    I remained an amused,
   bemused admirer.
   Time passed, as it does,
   waysides were fallen
   by and down, and I struck
   up a fiendship (sic) with
   John Boy Green the band's
   friend, confidante, driver,
   whipping boy and eminence
   grease, in short their
   roadperson. Drunken
   encounters and revolted
   fascination led to the notion
   that I should accompany the
clashers on their second, longest, American

tour as a sort of warped observer, war artist
(in Joe's words, apparently), witness and
bewildered bystander. Why not? Carrol
'Junior' Smith, Elvis' cousin had gone along
on the Memphis Flash's early forays into
the far side of insanity, who was I to deny
the call of the wild?
I witnessed the chaps putting the finishing
touches to some of the tracks that would
eventually comprise the London Calling album
down at Wessex Studios one sun drenched
metropolitan evening and the next
morning we were heading out over
the Atlantic on Flight 287 to
the (com)promised land and
points due west. Sample conversation
in flight - "As soon as I saw you
I thought you were some kind of
band. You know the band Jigsaw?
They're an English band." Addressed
to, and ignored by Green. The
words "mortal fear" and "drunk"
also figure in my notes from the
time.
Inevitably, the rapscallion Green
and I ended up in babbling mode
gazing down at the endless miles ▶
Mister Jones arrives at the Airport
waiting area.

* American Slang for 'Gang-Fight'
The Big Rumble*
DIGIT BOOKS
R360
DIGIT
2/6
A NEW SHOCKER OF MODERN YOUTH

of Americana rolled along below the mighty Boeing, the kind lady stewardesses having plied our hapless selves with free liquor.

Our first port of call after disembowel-ing at San Francisco was the Mission Ranch down Monterey way, a sort of bunkhouse, roadhouse, hotel for wayfaring wayfarers and after an exhausted sleep of the jetlagless and jetlegless I was up bright and early the next A.M., on the wild beaches of Carmel, California.

After rehearsals in a studio on Cannery row the band's first appearance was on the Monterey festival stage on a massive two day bill featuring past and past it luminaries like Dan Hicks, Country Joe and the Fish, Al Kooper and Big Mamma Thornton. This was the only time

JOE

WESSEX studios

BIll PRACE
Chief Stoker At WESSEX
Studios.

BEACHSide PAd - CARMEL Calif.
I ever saw the Clash play in bright noontime
sunshine and on a stage that seemed as vast
and forbidding as the deck of the Titanic.
The Strummer man unnerved me as he rushed
at me sidestage midway into the set pulling
horrible faces and pointing at his bloody
throat! I was trying to look as though I belonged
to the whole circus and his bizarre gesticulations
were as incomprehensible to me as if he were a
whirling dervish. It transpired that the poor
fellow's voice was shot and he needed a blast
of his honey and Special Brew (not) throat
soother. Rock and bleddy roll, what?
After the show we wandered the "fairground"

Elevator Goin' up!!..

MUSICIAN

S.D.

BOO

TRIBAL STOMP
MONTEREY FAIRGROUNDS

taking in the sights
and smells of the
colourful throng of the
mostly rather hippie-
fried Californians.
Mr. Wavy Gravy was
present being himself
in person. Was it him
wearing the angel
wings, my memory
falters? The ghosts
of Janis, Jimmi,
Jim and old Brian
Jones grimaced
and moved through
the fair.
The rest of the
tour happily deg-
-enerated into a
marathon slog of the length and breadth of the
Union aboard a homely old battlebus named
Arpeggio. Sweating and straining all over the
sprawling plains and through the claustrophobic
city canyons we fetched up at a giant ice rink
in Minneapolis/St. Paul for the first serious shows
of the journey.
The St. Pauls Civic Centre was so vast that
the band's equipment truck was parked up ▶

18

inside the place when we arrived. Kosmo Vynil and Andrew King (the money bag man from Blackhill Enterprises, then looking after the Clash's interests) had by now joined the circus. Andrew was the bag man holding or withholding the money, Kosmo's function eluded me, then and now. After intense rehear- -sals and sound- -checking through the 11th September, the band played the biggest event I'd witnessed them handle thus far. ▶

The Yankee audience were noisily anticipatory and the Clash didn't dissappoint them. The crowds of well wishers I spoke to after the Minneapolis shows were largely rapturous in their praise and boisterous admiration. Another win for the boys supported this time by the Undertones. Feargal to audience "I'm not English and I'm proud of it". Cheers.

By the 14th we have rolled into Chigaco where I remember a poor pissed-off polish lady telling me of her dissaffection with her life in the eni-town and her drudge-like existence at the Holiday Inn we stayed in. A pissed-off hotel chambermaid, reflecting the grey weather the couple of days we were there.

Bo-the man-Diddley showed up to rock the rafters in a baroque old theatre who'se name has vanished into the mists of my personal antiquity. I do recall the heaving masses rolling around stage front when the Clash got into their stride and I noted that paul lumbered around like a disconnected Frankenstein's monster in danger of crashing into anything sentient in his way. He became oddly feminine, however when he swayed into his own spotlight number, "The Guns of Brixton."

By the end of the first evening the scene was Babylonian, the audience a seething mass of debauched extras in a terribly venal Cecil B. DeMille gusset buster.

Chicago was also notable for a jaunt to WAXTRAX record store where I picked up the soon-to-be totemic "Elvis Presley" album (Rock and Roll No. 1), the pink and green woowzer that had so impressed me a hundred or so years earlier as the most down and dirty rock and roll album cover that was ever thrown together. Battered and scratched but unbowed, the vinyl bore a sticker on the runout groove saying $3. Plays Well. It did and still does, actually. I gazed on that inspirational cover shot taking daily doses of it's wasted genius.

The motor city was our next port of call, the Masonic Temple in down and dirty Detroit being the venue du jour, 11th September 1979, in the year of our liquid lunch. I remember musty old corridors with ancient group shots of cops, football players, dignitaries and

UNKNOWN MAN No.1.

ancient Masonic types gazing down across the ages to this dusty, sun-lit afternoon. God rest you gents and I wish I could have swiped some of your likenesses but some of the cops in those photo's looked forbidding in the extreme.

The town still seemed heavy industrial at that time with smoky skylines and a workman-like industrial buzz in the air. Oddly though I saw my first side-walk black blues picker there, singing his heart out to hurrying, indifferent Detroisese.

Detroit, is, of course a rockers town and the Clash went down accordingly well. Mick later jammed somewher or dranken other with the Motor City 5's own Wayne Kramer y'all.

A detour to Boston took us to the Orpheum theatre for a show on the 19th. A middle of the night arrival at a mildewed old hotel with long, gloomy corridors where the management didn't seem to expect ourselves, or perhaps anybody else. Tired flopalong with many of the crew in a dingy room.

By day Boston seemed a little more human in scale than some of our stops and after an afternoon soundchecking where I observed at length the boys attention to the details of their set they didn't dissappoint themselves and the charged up Beanites.

New York, Noo Yoik received the Clash like royalty on the 20th but the evening found Mr. Strummer in a bilious mood (it got to us all from time to time). Our man went a little wobbly in the dressing room, hurling a rather heavy glass ashtray at no one in particular before sinking into himself and curling into an unnapproachable lump of angst in a corner seat. His ever present golfriend of the time, the estimable Gabby tried to lure him back to placid waters. By showtime all was repaired and the boys had a great time, bringing punk to the punkocracy. Someone had located a candleabra somewhere backstage and Joe appropriated it for a dramatic if somewhat hamlike entrance for 'Armagideon Time.' The ▶

NEW YORK ... new YORK

28

boy swayed on stage with the candles lit and flickering, a single pale spot eventually illuminating his progress. Kosmo's influence, perhaps? While in New York we spoke of making a new stage backdrop to replace the tired old flags of all nations number they were hauling around. I obtained the requisite amount of rough canvas and numerous large tins of industrial paints and began the ultimately fruitless task of trying to locate a space big enough to paint something. I'd worked out a couple of skyline type backdrops and was ready to go but all leads proved in vain. I mostly recall one stinking Saturday afternoon in the pouring rain hustling around to various addresses of lofts and the like, paint cans in tow, and only connecting with avaricious bastards who wanted exorbitant payments, upfront.

No deal of course, so no freaking back-drop was ever done and God only knows where the paints and canvas ended up. A solo flight to somewhere or other followed for me. Nervous but becoming blasé by now. If the Clash weren't going down in a blazing air wreck then none of the party were either. Also helped by the fact that jumping on a plane in the U.S.A. was like getting a bus over here ▶

◀ Lensperson Ms. Pennie Smith.

ALL LOST IN THE WHADAYAMACALLIT

Somehow we are all together again for the crossing
into Canada. Waiting, much waiting at immigr-
-ation until our passports are stamped and we
are busing it on to Toronto, stopping at the
Niagra Falls and photographs by Pennie Smith
who is now aboard the ship of fools along with
Paul Morley, sent over by Neil Spencer at the NME
to add to the ballast. Pennie and I share travel
sickness pills, occassional hotel rooms and a love
for the vainglorious quest we are embarked on.
              We shared a nauseous, hungover
(on my part) afternoon in Philadelphia lying

on our beds watching an old black and white
movie about the sinking of the Titanic and
discussing the English 'underground' scene and
the deceased magazines we had variously
contributed to. Grey day in Philly where a bunch
of us went along to catch
Apocalypse Now at a local cinema.
I found it then, as now, a hugely
overrated piece of bunkum with
no insights whatsoever into the
nature of the Vietnamese fight and
pitifully inadequate as some kind
of filmic 'Heart of Darkness' Roll
over Joe Conrad.
Back to Canada and Pennie
had snapped our men
cavorting around in
front of the roaring ▶

Falls lurching around in their cutesy snap brim hats bought in the Windy City. Mr. Porkpie calling. Mingus ah-um.

The played a couple of nights at the O'Keefe Centre in Toronto opening the set with Vince Taylor's 'Brand New Cadillac' and not looking back. The rabid Torontans managed to invade the stage at one point. By now the front line were all greased up and way beyond their so--called 'punk' origins, visually, sartorially, musically. (In a despatch back to the old NME I described them as resembling the 'bastard offspring of Gene Vincent out of Eddie Cochran crossed with a Harley Davidson motorsickel' and, by golly, they did.

One of my drawings from Toronto bears the caption "Done when drunk again. This is shit." The modus operandi was to do quick sketches backstage or down in the audience and work them up with coloured inks back in various hotel rooms

Unknown Woman No.1

Mick J. and Joe.

THE CLASH

late into the night. While drunk. This cannot
be faulted as a young man's working method.
Except that I was a decade older than most
everyone else on the road, Whiskers Green
being about half a decade behind me, so far.

The 25th found us in Montreal at
the Orpheum Theatre where the stage was
again invaded when Joe stormed into "White
Riot." Just like the far off days in England. A
distant memory by now.

Another sweaty bus trek and we were
back over the border for a show at the Clark
University in Worcester Massachusets which was
notable for the fact that the place was surrounded
by armed police at one point early in the even-
-ing (for why?). Mr Green had to gain access to
our hotel by smashing the glass door to
reception with his "atomic pink", it says here.

flightcase, to general delight. I think it was here that finances became so desperate that Mr. Pete Silverton of now defunct 'Sounds' rock rag had his credit card pressed into service to pay the bill. How unlike the home life of our own dear Fab Four. The Ritchie Colloseum (Colosseum?) in a suburb of the other Washington (Maryland) was next for the taking and Screaming Jay Hawkins was support complete with his coffin. A tad theatrical for me, I confess. Lots of drawing opportunities down in the audience for this one. Sometimes it was just too frantic and one had to go back sidestage for elbow room, but it was always salutory to hear and see the crowds face to face.

Memories blur and recollection goes into hyperdrive now. I am on my own (bliss) on a sunny morning in Atlanta Georgia lounging on a piece of dappled grass (and in the middle of the city. People, mostly black, drift around, lounging and generally horsing about on this most beautiful of days, the 1st October 1979. A day later the Clash lay into the audiences at the Agora ballroom but today is for rest and wandering. Atlanta is a bigger, more spacious place than most of our stops so far. To me it has a distinctly less frantic edge and I have drifted into a largely black neighbourhood without noticing any distinct transition. Later ▶

Atlanta 42 1/10

38

Pennie and I explore the streets
and the gay crowded places
discovering edge of town
thrift stores of unimaginable
delights. She buys an art-deco
airplane lamp for resident
jester Kosmo and I settle for
a vastly oversized white
jacket of the type favoured
by Sir Sid in the "My Way"
section of the Great R' and R
swindle.
The Agora ballroom is the venue
on the 2nd. and most of the
black and white sketches in
this booklet were done there-
-abouts.
Nights and days were hotter and
more oppressive the further
south the old bus travailed but
Texas was something else
entirely. We jetted in to Dallas
or Huston while Major Tom
steered the old faithful and some
of the crew to our next destin-
-ations. The air was like a great
humid blanket wrapping itself
around us as we deplaned in
blazing sunlight.

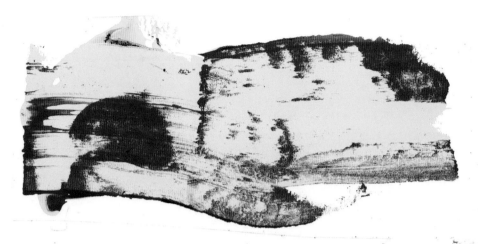

Dallas was memorable for our trip to Dealey Plaza to see the road curve in front of the most infamous book depository. Kosmo saw fit to despoil any gravitas the occassion might have nurtured in our souls by lying down in the gutter pretending dead. Ha ha...you can take the boy out of Sarfend etc. Joe saw fit to display his gnarled old gnashers to me at the same spot. I can't remember what enquiry might have triggered this but the sight was nothing less than wince inducing. People have compared rows of bombed out houses to rotting teeth, with Joe his mouth was a small towns worth of blackened bombed out houses. Some gob.

The actual venues played in those first southern forays seem to have slipped from memory and my drawing books. I know that Rory had joined us by then. He had worked with John Rotten and company on their southern lurches and Joe soon had him converted into a fully greased up member of the party.

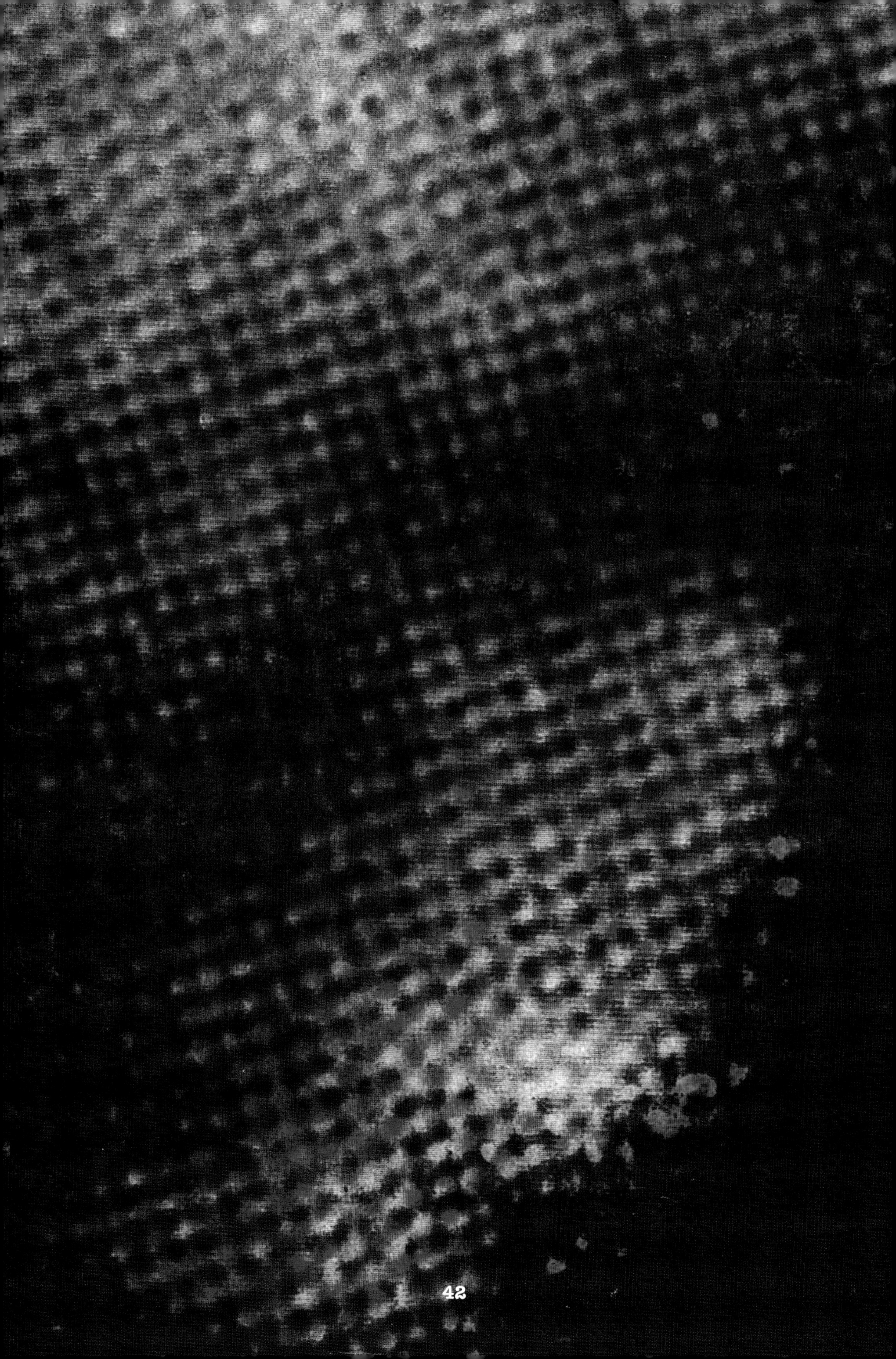

I had first referred to it as the "stains on the pillow tour" in New York and the chaps had been leaving hair gloop skidmarks all over the States. In the south I picked up the sine qua non of hair wax. An odourous concoction called 'Tres Flores' with a sickly sweet hint of hawthorn and something indefinable and jarred up, oddly enough, in New Jersey. Marvellous stuff, so poignant and delicate that one could imagine a bunch of consumptive fin-de-siecle delicates reciting Keats and studying Beardsley drawings while idly grooming their hair with the stuff.

I plastered it on to ludicrous effect and sweated through night town Huston and Dallas.

Austin called us from afar. We entombed ourselves in a delightfully air-conditioned slab at one end of town and I ventured into the wonderful breathless Texas evenings. Thinking to finally sample the tipple said to be a regular hit for old Gene Vincent I entered a large and empty liquor store just down the main drag and sought to purchase a bottle of Thunderbird wine, to be chagrined by the owner's request that I return with my passport as proof of my age. I was thirty four at the time.

Austin then, and maybe still, was a home from home for multifarious good old boys, weirdos

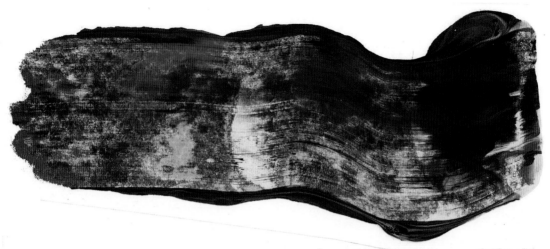

and rock and rollers. Cars were parked wild-west fashion, noses to the sidewalk like tied up horses. A lovely place all in all, on a shopping foray I picked up some hot-diggity brand new old-fashioned style 501's, the last authentic pair I ever encountered. Jam productions Inc., of San Antonio had the Clash booked into the Armadillo World Headquarters for the 4th October and the night was the most genuine and one of the most rockingest of the tour.

It was still daylight when Joe and company began belting it out. The venue was a delight-fully homey old wooden structure (in memory at least, inside anyway, The floor hopefully) and beer was served up in those enormous pitchers beloved of honky tonks and good time drinking establishments. Joe Ely had turned up. This vastly talented and underrated Lubbock maverick was Joe's special compadre and the two seemed to have a mutual

Good MoRnin' Little Schoolgirl...

admiration society like
the co-operative whole-
-sale and Ely jammed
easily with the band,
locking on to strummer's
rockabilly roots and love
of country music. Here
and later in London the
two Joe's cut an usual
pair. Mr E., always in cow-
-boy boots, bootlace, collar
points and the inevitable
stetson and Mr. Strum'
sliding ever further to
the Vince Taylor end of the
fashion spectrum.
I stole a big Coors pitcher
and carried it safely back
to England, my token of
a rocking time in Texas.
   Joe Ely was one of the
high plains boys from Lubbock
home of the great bespec-
-tacled hornswaggler, good
old Buddy Holly. We all
had our totally shredded
nights when nothing
but oblivion would do
and my night of fear hit
in Lubbock, causing me ▶

Bus boredom....

to miss a San Diego
show and an unsch-
-eduled visit to good
old Buddy's grave.
Instead I sweated
through nightmares
in the Holiday Inn.
I was well enough
next day and I did
a couple of drawings
out in the endless
sun waiting for
departure time.
Mr. Ely hove by in
his pink limousine.
I think they call it
living the life.
Well, goodbye
Joe, me gotta go,
me oh my oh, and
the 9th October
found me drawing
scenes on the old
bus and the view
of the baking
sands and desolate
gas stations on
the road to Lost
Angeles and the
Sunset Marquis ▷

LUBBOCK calling,

hotel. This, they told us was 'the' rock and roll hotel of fantastic L.A. whatever.

Days of comparat--ive leisure followed. We met up again with Mo', the slightly frazzled Vietnam veteran who J.G. had known from other times and had greeted us earlier in Monterey. He and I took a ride San Francisco a couple of days furth--er on into the West coast and had our handwrit--ing analysed by a very perceptive lady at some fair. Johnny G., hated Los Angeles and I think it was here-abouts that he ▶

checked himself briefly into some hospital with something like a suspected ulcer. He was out again the same day and we did a frenzied round of all the touristy bits and pieces. I managed to vomit quietly somewhere near to the old Hollywood sign way up in the hills, a combination of car rides, heat and booze finally leading to a technicolour upchuck. I glimpsed some of the star signs on Hollywood Boulevard and i'm told I was present when Joe insisted on running his fingers through the still extant bullet holes marking the site of John Dillinger's final appointment with lead outside the Biograph Theatre.

Joe, Johnny and myself had an enduring fascination with criminal psychopaths and lunatic killers. Charles Starkweather figured in our iconography as much as Buddy or Elvis. One day the man just flips, starts shooting and the rest is outlaw history. Actual photographs of Bonnie and Clyde Barrow's auto' after the fatal ambush reveal nothing more nor less than your common or garden rock and rollmobile. The entire contents of their wardrobe hang out of the bullet-riddled doors and lie scattered around with papers, cases, handbags and the daily detritus of a life less ordinary. The scene of Eddie Cochran's fatal meeting with a Chippenham lamp-post

was described similarly by witnesses on the scene early - the battered roof, doors gaping open on the doomed Ford Consul, sheet music flying everywhere, a bleeding body on the grass and the awful silence. Plus the streetlights all went out.

Back in L.A., I trudged around on foot defying the stultifying car culture of the sprawl. Jim Morrison best captures the suffocating null-ness of Lost Angeles, the skull behind the ready smile. I spent the early evening of Thursday (11th October in a sweaty rush around a vast Tower Records store trying to locate the original cast recording of 'West Side Story! Joe loved a theme or motif for every event and tonight he wanted Barry Myers our on-road Deejay to blast out "Gee, officer Krupki" before the band hit the boards. Corny beyond belief. I had suggested and received the blessing for the playing of "The Shape I'm In" at the New York shows. At least it was within spitting distance of rock and roll, courtesy of beach beauty Johnny Restivo. Before you knock it cop it blasting over the waltzers on a funfair one summer evening in 1959. Boy, did they let it rock.

         I noticed albums of Hitler's Nuremberg rally speeches in Tower's environs. That would have been a sensational opener for us, but ▶

I had but enough dollars, courtesy of Blackhill Ents., to purchase the requested item. Always the gofer, never the gofed.

Thursday 11th October, baking heat in the Hollywood Palladium and Country Joe Ely has turned up again to support the Rockabilly Rebels and the Clash. The air is febrile with barely suppressed hysteria. These dingbats have come to see the latest English sensation and they want it now!

The Rebels look the rocking end but to these ears remained an essentially ham-fisted revivalist bunch, like the Stray Cats

59

without the blown-up
cartoon pretensions.
One of Joe Ely's band is
moved to produce a dust-
bin full of iced water
which is hurled over
the front rows of the
audience to cool their
fervour.
The Clash eventually
appeared, to shred what's
left of the tattered collective consciousness and
once again ragged elements
of the front line make
the stage, staggering
around like shell-shocked
survivors of a machine
gun charge while the
band try to continue.
Strange, the need to
disrupt what one is
ostensibly enjoying and
equally strange to whip
an audience into such
frenzies and then ask
for collective calm to
descend.
Early footage of the ▶

Clash playing in Munich, available as an extra on, the 'RUDE BOY' DVD, perfectly captures the sort of madness they were capable of unleashing on a hot night. It's awesomely pow--erful and catches them at the very peak of their powers. BACK ON THE ROAD AGAIN - see opposite; we scarfed up the miles all the way to Seattle, while the band flew on ahead. It was either there, or further on that a bunch of Pennie's contact sheets arrived and the minor skirmish over which photograph would finally grace the LONDON CALLING cover was res-.olved. Thank you Mr. Strummer for your support and encouragement. I light a candle to your memory every year. It's true, I sure do. Seattle was a refreshing change after the heat of the south.

We stayed at the same seafront hotel earlier made infamous by the piscatorial activies of one of the Led Zeppelin crowd. Nice way to treat a woman, but then, the poor boy maybe never had a woman of his own. Or even a mother. The town I liked a lot - the closeness of the sea after all that sodding desert, fresh fish, civilized book- -stores, even a freight railroad track run- -ning nearly through the middle of town. I went for long walks a lot of the time, as the rock and roll slog was beginning to, ▶

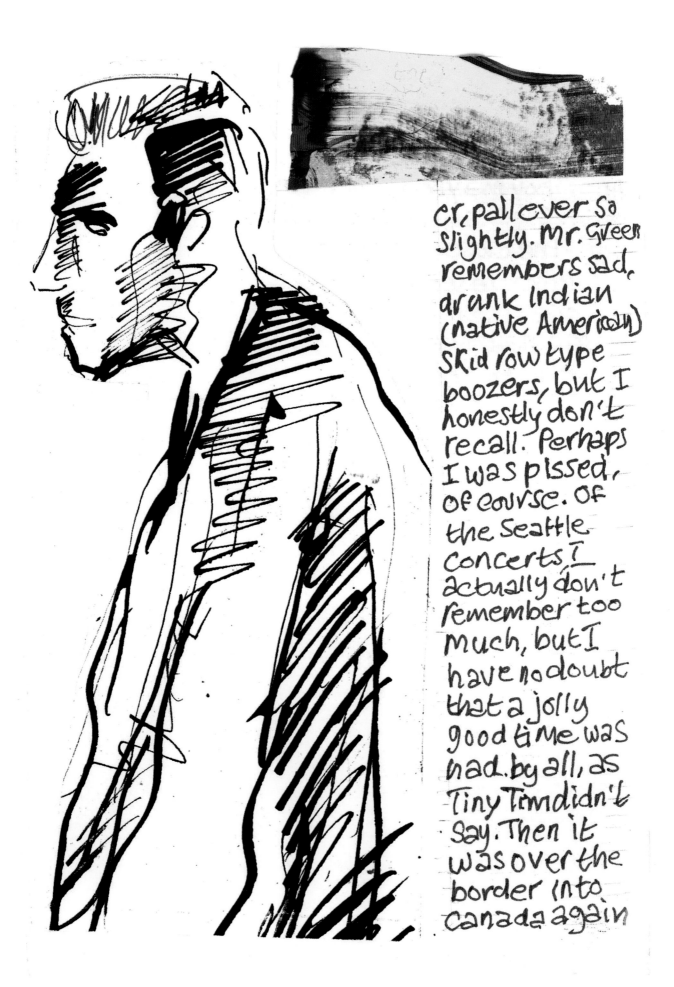

er, pall ever so slightly. Mr. Green remembers sad, drunk Indian (native American) skid row type boozers, but I honestly don't recall. Perhaps I was pissed, of course. Of the Seattle concerts, I actually don't remember too much, but I have no doubt that a jolly good time was had. by all, as Tiny Tim didn't say. Then it was over the border into Canada again

We weren't sure when we arrived, but Vancouver prove to be the bitter end of our jaunt. There had been vague tales of continueing down to Cuba or maybe El Salvador but the seeds of collapse seemed to have entered our very souls and rumours were heard about strife within the band. How true they proved to be, eventually. ~~the~~ I met up with an old pen friend, Ms., Debbie Dawson who I cruelly ignored in later years when I became involved with the one and ex-Mrs., Lowry. I ducked into a local library before the "gig" and refreshed my own

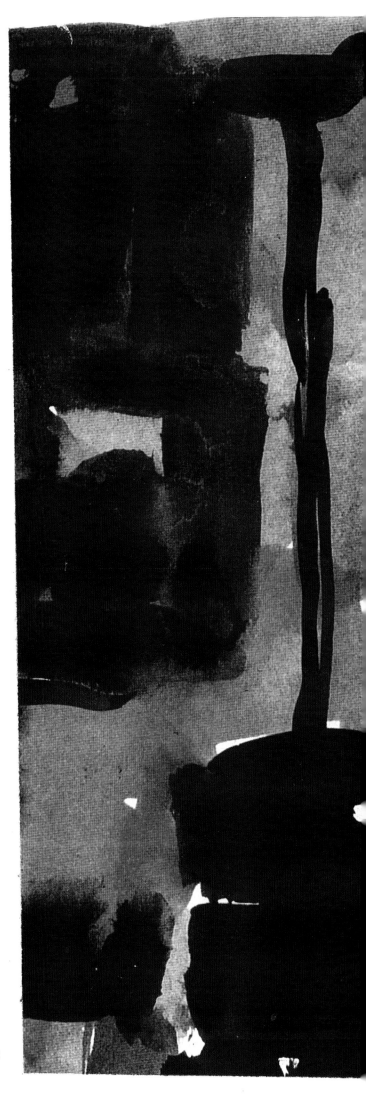

THE CLASH

arid soul with a couple of chapters of a Patricia
Highsmith novel. Whatever, the show was
terrific, the boys were on form and I apologise
to a Mr. Bob Rock of Vancouver for never
sending him the pair of Brothel creepers I
rashly promised him that I would, in the exub-
-erence of the hour. Quite a night, down in
the audience, suffused with joy.
The morning was a vastly different carton
of fish, however. Everyone seemed to have
woken with a sense of dread. Rumours flew
of open arguments between various band
members and some of us seemed to grasp
that this was the time for flight. I don't

CONTS. 3 PAGES ALONG ▶

REHEARSALS—
BLOODY REHEARSALS.

MONTREAL.

RAINY DAY WOMEN
12 AND 35.

exactly remember in
what mode of transport we
reached the airport, may-
-be our heels became winged
but Johnny Green, his wife
Lindy (who had joined us in
New York) Warren Steadman,
the lighting man and perhaps
Barry Myers the on-tour
deejay, found ourselves

happily and safely
seated in a bloody big
jet leaving the madness
behind and far below.
Roll them engines big boy
and take us safely home.
On arrival at Heathrow we
were greeted by a big black
old limousine. Johnny and
Lindy to an eventual holiday
to somewhere remote and
restful (not a chance). I
went north for some

beer and recuperation. All too soon, though this idyll was over and I was sucked back into the mad, bad world of..........

LONDON

LUBBOCK CALLING

JOE ELY
JIMMIE DALE GILMORE
BUTCH HANCOCK
MORE

THE CLASH

THE "LONDON CALLING" ALBUM COVER HAD TO FEATURE THE INFAMOUS PINK AND GREEN ROCK AND ROLL LETTERING. GOD MADE ME DO THAT. EARLY ROUGHS SHOW THAT AS THE ONE CONSTANT WITH

SAY, THE BAND ROUGHLY DE-
-LINIATED, DEPENDING UPON
WHICH PHOTO' WAS EVENTUALLY
TO DROP FROM HEAVEN. JOE
WOULD OFTEN LOOK OVER MY
SHOULDER, AS WOULD MICHAEL,
AND MR. STRUMMER THOROUGHLY
APPROVED OF MY CHOICE, AS HE
MADE QUITE OBVIOUS. EVERYTHING
WAS DONE ON A WINK AND A NOD
BASIS AND WHY THE HELL I THOUGHT
I WAS EVEN GOING TO GET NEAR
TO THE COVER IS A BIT OF A
MYSTERY. SOD IT, LET'S JUST HAVE
A GO. WE COULDN'T DO WORSE
THAN HIPGNOSIS, GOD HELP US...

I BELIEVE THAT JOE AND I WERE
THE ONLY ONES TO SHARE THAT
EXULTANT "YIHAA! THIS IS IT" MOMENT
WHEN WE SPOTTED THAT MARVELLOUS
LITTLE SHOT AMONG THE MANY,
MANY SHOTS ON PENNIE'S SHEET OF
CONTACT PRINTS ONE SHADY, SMOKEY
EVENING IN SOME HOTEL IN SOME
STATE, TOWARDS THE END OF THE
TRIP. I DIDN'T KNOW UNTIL JUST
RECENTLY THAT THE DEAR CHAP
HAD WRANGLED LONG AND HARD WITH
PENNIE ABOUT IT. THE OLD GAL
DIDN'T FANCY IT BECAUSE IT WAS
OBVIOUSLY OUT-OF-FOCUS, BUT I THINK
THAT HIS STRUMMERSHIP AND MOI
SAW A FANTASTIC ROCKING MOMENT,

MONSIEUR SIMONON SMASHING THE
TOOL OF HIS TRADE TO SMITHEREENS
ON THE STAGE OF THE NEW YORK
PALLADIUM — POW! — TAKE THAT
YOU YANKEE UPSTARTS — WE'RE STILL
SO BORED WITH THE U.S.A.
ACTUALLY I HAD NO IDEA THAT IT
WAS OUT OF FOCUS. HALF BLIND AT
THE BEST OF TIMES AND PROBABLY
HALF PISSED AT THE TIME, THAT
SIMPLY HAD TO BE THE ONE. HISTORY
SEEMS TO HAVE PROVED US CORRECT
BUT; BACK THEN, IT SEEMED THAT
THE COMBINATION OF THE RIP-OFF
LETTERING AND AN UNRECOGNIZABLE
CENTRAL FIGURE WOULD CAUSE ALL
SORTS OF DIFFICULTIES WITH THE

POWERS THAT BE'D AT C.B.S. WE
NEED NOT HAVE WORRIED. MY DESIGN
AND MYSELF WERE MET WITH SOME
-THING A LITTLE SHORT OF INDIFFERENCE
BACK IN LONDON AND I WAS CON —
-FINED TO THE OBSCURITY OF SOME
CORNER IN THEIR ART DEPARTMENT
WHILE THE BIG BOYS EXCITED THEM-
-SELVES WITH THE THEN, LATEST
SHAKIN' STEVENS SLICE OF VYNIL
REGURGITATION. I SEEM TO RECALL
RADIO 1 BEING ON MOST OF THE
TIME. NOM DU MERDE! WE WHO
WOULD VALIANT BE ETC, ETC..
JOE'S ONLY OTHER CONTRIBUTION
WAS HIS STIPULATION ON A MATT
FINISH TO THE PICTURE. OH WELL,

THESE BOYS ALL HAVE THEIR IDEO-
-SINCRACIES AND I HAD HAD A NICE
STATESIDE HOLIDAY. WE PUSHED THE
BUGGER THROUGH — ONLY REGRET,
THE PINK WASN'T QUITE HOT ENOUGH.
FLUORESCENT WOULD HAVE BEEN NICE,
BUT I STILL FELT THAT I WAS WALKING
ON THIN ICE. MONSEWER GREEN
AND I, REUNITED, MADE ODD TRIPS
TO THE PRINTERS, JUST TO MAKE SURE
THAT THEY WEREN'T PUTTING SHAKIN'
STEVENS ON THE COVER. THE OLD
BOY EVEN SUGGESTED TO ME, RECENTLY
THAT THEY SHOULD ERECT A "LONDON
CALLING" SIGN INSTEAD OF THE TIRED
OLD HOLLYWOOD SIGN. NEAT BLOODY
IDEA, WHEN YOU COME TO THINK

OF IT !!. THE SAME MR. GREEN ON HEARING I'M LEAVING.. THE FIRST SANDINISTA TRACK OF SPRING

HELL

AHEM... I AM AWARE OF FOUR OR FIVE PAST- -CHES OF OUR OWN DEAR "PASTICHE", THE LATEST, AND MOST BLATANT

BEING THE K.D. LANG ALBUM—
WOOPS!! FORGOTTEN THE TITLE AND I
SURE AIN'T BUYING THE MUTHA. NON,
IMITATION IS THE SINCEREST FORM OF
FLATTERY, AS I TOLD THE KING WHEN
HE CAME AFTER ME WITH A BARETTA,
BUT, MY DEAR LADY, YOUR DESIGNER
HASN'T GOT THE DYNAMIC OR, MOST
IMPORTANTLY, THE BALANCE OF THE
DESIGN CORRECT. THE PHOTOGRAPH
JUST DOESN'T INTERACT PROPERLY
WITH THE LETTERING. QUEL HORREUR!
STUDY OUR OWN EFFORT, OR MORE
PERTINENTLY THE ORIGINAL, AND STILL
THE BEST. EVERYTHING WORKS. ONLY
CONNECT DEAR, OR IN YOUR CASE,
CORRECT. SHOOT THE DESIGNER!!

MS. SMITH - SHOOTEUR TO THE STARS CAME AFTER ME WITH A ZOOM LENS WHEN I HAD THE TEMERITY TO "TRIM" HER ORIGINAL PICTURE BUT IT HAD TO BE DONE, FOR THE SAKE OF SERENDIPITY. STUDY THE DESIGN OF THE 'SANDINISTA' COVER - "OH GOD, NO, DON'T. DOES IT WORK? DOES IT HECK. CUT, CUT, CUT. FEAR-LESSLY AND FOR THE SAKE OF YOUR ART AND FUTURE · REPUTATION. IN MY CASE AS A FEARLESS BULLSHITTER AND "NO SHOW" MERCHANT. DID HANK WILLIAMS BOTHER TO TURN UP FOR MANY OF HIS OWN GIGS. OF COURSE NOT. HOW PLEBIAN! HOW RECHERCHE!! HOW TOO BLOODY TOO. I'M REMINDED OF THE FAMOUS CHE GUEVARA PICTURE.

BOREDOM AND PARANOIA... TORONTO.
1979

So how did you get to play with Eddie Cochran?
Originally we were to back Gene Vincent. I knew all the Cliff Gallup solos. But then Eddie released Hallelujah I Love Her So and it was a hit, so he was more the star. So Larry switched us. Didn't know much about Eddie, except that he played everything on his records. So Brian Bennett looked forward to it because there were some innovative drum patterns on Eddie's records. Rock drumming was basically boom-boom-chick, you know.

So we went to the rehearsal rooms and he seemed a really nice guy. Leather trousers, orange shirt, black waistcoat – and make-up! He showed Brian a few things on drums – never heard anything like it. Then he picked up the bass – wow! And of course on guitar he was superb. I asked him about Chet Atkins, and the first thing he taught me was Birth Of The Blues, Chet Atkins style, with all these nice jazz chords. He was a good flat-top picker as well. Not the greatest blues player, perhaps – on Milk Cow Blues he did exactly the same intro and solo every night. But he was still good enough to make our eyes pop!

Is it true that Cochran taught you to use light strings to bend the note?
No. Joe Brown said that, but I already had unwound strings. I had experimented with a banjo first and second, and moved everything else down. Light and ~ndy. But it was James Burton who gave me the ~a, not Eddie. Bending one note into another – he fantastic.

other memories do you have of the 1960 tour?
~n learned that Gene was a thug. There were ~en he'd threaten someone with a knife.

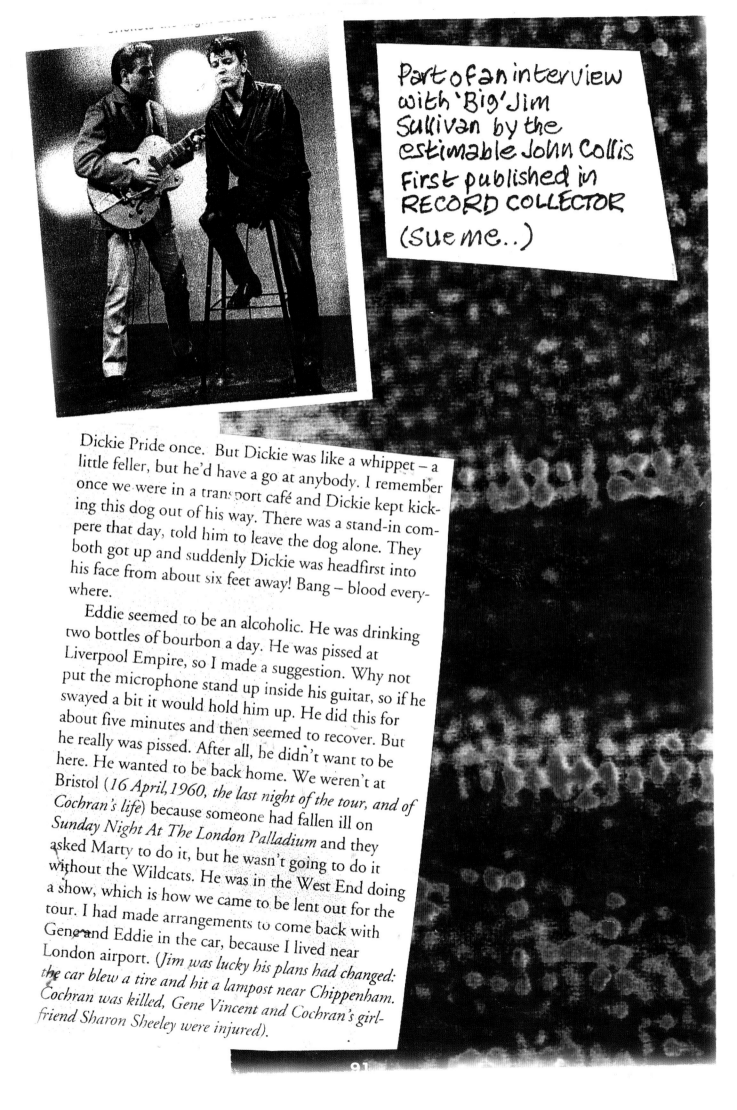

Dickie Pride once. But Dickie was like a whippet – a little feller, but he'd have a go at anybody. I remember once we were in a transport café and Dickie kept kicking this dog out of his way. There was a stand-in compere that day, told him to leave the dog alone. They both got up and suddenly Dickie was headfirst into his face from about six feet away! Bang – blood everywhere.

Eddie seemed to be an alcoholic. He was drinking two bottles of bourbon a day. He was pissed at Liverpool Empire, so I made a suggestion. Why not put the microphone stand up inside his guitar, so if he swayed a bit it would hold him up. He did this for about five minutes and then seemed to recover. But he really was pissed. After all, he didn't want to be here. He wanted to be back home. We weren't at Bristol (*16 April, 1960, the last night of the tour, and of Cochran's life*) because someone had fallen ill on *Sunday Night At The London Palladium* and they asked Marty to do it, but he wasn't going to do it without the Wildcats. He was in the West End doing a show, which is how we came to be lent out for the tour. I had made arrangements to come back with Gene and Eddie in the car, because I lived near London airport. (*Jim was lucky his plans had changed: the car blew a tire and hit a lampost near Chippenham. Cochran was killed, Gene Vincent and Cochran's girlfriend Sharon Sheeley were injured*).

THE MADNESS OF
KING JOE, R.I.P.

Truthfully, I didn't see a lot of the boys after the tour. I stayed briefly with Joe and Gabbi in Fulham designing the singles sleeves and then I headed back north, not wanting to seem a parasite or a psychophant. Joe Strummer was a very special individual and maybe I should have kept in touch, but, naw... the boy was busy....

God bless you, old man, wherever you are. And wherever you are... give my regards to Eddie.

JAM Productions, Inc.

SAN ANTONIO, TEXAS

THE CLASH

ARMADILLO WORLD HEADQUARTERS

OCTOBER 4, 1979

Ya should have been there!!

AuThor!!.. AuthoR !!..
ARThuR...

No animals were hurt in the making of this production.

Words by Ben Myers

Many words have been written about The Clash since they took rock music by the throat in **1976** and gave a tired, complacent industry the shock of its life. If disaffected youths were at first seduced by the band's combination of **style** and **attitude**, Britain's rock journalists were captivated more by its urgent music, its varied influences and its **overtly political** stance. In an age when the inky music papers - particularly The Melody Maker and the NME - were rock kingmakers, The Clash were soon front page news. They were, and I suppose it's a contradiction in terms, **punk aristocracy**.

The Clash were not only **key players** in the birth of UK punk, but they also helped take it around the world. They broke America - a feat that that they themselves would surely have thought impossible to achieve during those heady early days of **the punk movement**. Perhaps they also wouldn't have much cared. Yet in their hands, somehow music that sounded so **parochial** managed to travel the globe.

Now, with punk long dead and gone, The Clash have taken their place in the pantheon of rock gods, sitting ironically alongside bands whose influence and reputations they originally set out to destroy - The Beatles, The Rolling Stones, Led Zeppelin and the rest.

Like all the great bands, they've influenced many that followed; The Clash twisted dub reggae, ska and rockabilly into new musical forms that inspired eighties bands such as The Specials and U2. Who can fail to hear echoes of The Clash in the music of Nirvana and Green Day? Surely the band's gang-like swagger and use of their home town as a lyrical muse can be heard in the songs of The Libertines and Arctic Monkeys. And that is just the tip of the iceberg. There are still countless bands, whether they're playing at the Dog and Ferret on a Friday night or headlining at Glastonbury, that acknowledge the debt they owe The Clash.

Above all though, there's a great story of a band that came out of nowhere and set the world alight - and looked great as they did it. Oh yes, and the small matter of a rich and enduring body of work that has withstood thirty years of musical fads and fashions.

Singer/guitarists Joe Strummer and Mick Jones, bassist Paul Simonon, and drummer Topper Headon were the self-styled 'Last Gang in Town'. They were also a mass of contradictions; a band whose biggest hit was a posthumous release off the back of a Levi's advert; a band who wanted to destroy rock 'n' roll but eventually became part of its establishment; a band whose recorded output features a fair few stinkers alongside the classics. But to me, this merely made The Clash seem all the more human. It was the effort that was appreciated - and after all, the music lives on.

Since the untimely death of Joe Strummer at the age of only 50 in 2002, interest in The Clash seems to have grown and grown. Mick Jones continues to perform and produce new bands, while Paul Simonon has recently resurfaced playing bass in Damon Albarn's band The Good, The Bad & The Queen - make no mistake, these guys are still successful. If they did no more work during their lives, though, they'd still have the satisfaction of knowing that they played in a band that spoke to a generation. How many musicians can say that?

Here, then, is one interpretation of the tale, and a lifelong fan's analysis of their music. I hope you enjoy it.

Ben Myers, Spring 2007

Whether you're a **lifelong devotee** who was there the first time around or a curious young fan taking your first steps into the scene by way of today's young bands, to really appreciate the power of punk you must surely first understand the band who mixed **art-school sensibilities** with **working-class** ideology and political protest, and a sense of rock 'n' roll history while keeping a firm eye on the future.

More than any other band, The Clash expanded punk's musical horizons by incorporating such other genres as reggae, dub, ska and rockabilly, and making it more than a souped-up three-chord thrash. That had been done memorably and successfully in the USA by The Ramones - there was no need to do it all over again in Britain. Even from their very early records you can hear the band's desire to push on musically and to combine invention with all the restless energy.

The Clash were the only band to emerge from the thrilling London punk scene in 1976 and 1977 to go truly global and to stick around long enough to enjoy it. The Sex Pistols gained the international notoriety, but they disintegrated after only one studio album, confirming for many of the old-guard critics that punk was the disposable flash-in-the-pan movement that they had always suspected it to be. They didn't count on The Clash.

Just as Liverpool looms large in the Beatles story, it's the grimy streets of England's capital city that is the backdrop to the songs of Joe Strummer and Mick

Jones. London is everywhere; you can almost taste it. London was The Clash's greatest inspiration.

The future members of the band were all born during the austere post-war period, when rationing was only just ending and many aspects of Britain had changed little since Victorian times. Rock 'n' roll and the creation of the 'teenager' as a visible demographic happened during their adolescence, and they all came of age in the late sixties and early seventies when London was placed firmly at the centre of the cultural universe.

The likes of the Beatles and the Stones had paved the way for a whole new generation of rock bands, a generation which had dissipated and diversified into many musical sub-genres united by a love of electricity: acid rock, psychedelia, progressive rock, folk-rock, heavy rock/metal, and glam/glitter rock.

So by the early seventies, Carnaby Street and the King's Road, symbols of the swinging sixties, had already begun to swing to a new beat. The Vietnam War had politicised the young, the hippy epoch had peaked with Woodstock and Altamont, and rock music was moving in different directions. Some directions were darker and heavier, as epitomised by such bands as Led Zeppelin, who strutted around the world like untouchable other-worldly gods; Yes, Genesis and similar bands took off on musical flights of fancy; and glam-rock arrived on a sea of face paint.

This was all well and good, but life for young men and women in the street was a far cry from the world of the stars presented in NME or on Top Of The Pops, who operated from their lofty pedestals before retreating to their country mansions or tax-dodging foreign retreats. There was little connection between the musician and those who bought the music.

The gap between music fan and rock star was as wide as it had ever been; it didn't involve the young fans, it kept them at arm's length. This situation made for the creation of some of the most self-indulgent, overblown rock music ever being put together and taken on tour at ludicrous cost by the privileged few who had been allowed into the old-boy network establishment that was the British music industry.

This is exactly where punk came in.

The argument as to when punk actually began still rages today, but let's start with two late-60s Detroit bands, the Stooges and MC5, who took rudimentary garage rock, amplified it, and turned it into something way more forceful, inspirational, volatile, and subversive than anything that had gone before. Their incendiary live performances were legendary, and though neither band sold many records, they did set a new standard for how far rock music could - and should - be pushed.

In New York, the Velvet Underground stripped things down and painted them black, while in their wake the New York Dolls bastardised the bluesy imprint of the Stones with a hard-edged - if shambolic - street-smart sound and flamboyant, confrontational presentation.

All these bands influenced those few visionaries who decided to take this disparate music to another level and no one took up the mantle with more enthusiasm than the Ramones, who burst out of the New York borough of Queens in 1974 and let their brilliance shine in their sound's utter simplicity. With three chords, energy in abundance, and a real 'don't-give-a stuff' attitude, they showed that a lack of money, good looks, and natural musical ability didn't have to get in the way of making exciting music played from the heart. The term 'punk' itself passed into everyday use via the fanzine of the same name that first documented this initial wave of such Ramones-affiliated-and-inspired bands emerging from New York clubs like CBGB's and Max's Kansas City. Import copies of albums by these bands filtered their way through to Britain, where the charts were largely ruled by inane pop-and-ballad bands or flares-wearing progressive rockers; this new sound had a life-changing effect on the culture-junkie future members of The Clash.

Before that, though, it was in the ethnically diverse and largely working-class South London areas of Streatham and Brixton, respectively, that Mick Jones and Paul Simonon (both born 1955) found their way into music through the Jamaican reggae and ska music that their classmates turned them onto. While Jones was also into such glam-leaning bands as the New York Dolls and Mott The Hoople, Simonon's love of ska and reggae led him to the mod and skinhead scenes, two defiantly working-class subcultures united by a love of black music and sharp clothes, two key factors that The Clash would incorporate from day one.

101

Both came from working-class origins and broken homes. Simonon's father was a member of the communist party, while Jones spent a large part of his teen years living with his grandmother Stella, in a West London tower block that overlooked the Westway, that Ballardian concrete flyover road that runs through and over the heart of the city.

"When I was pretty young my dad decided we didn't have to go to Catholic church any more, and went on to join the Communist party," Simonon told me in 2004. "But what I couldn't get was how come I was the one out delivering the leaflets and he was the one at home watching the telly! So I was aware of the political system early on and also, obviously, because I grew up listening to a lot of reggae, music that had more edge than a lot of contemporary music in terms of political content. To me, it seemed normal. For Joe [Strummer] it was folk music - people like Woody Guthrie or Bob Dylan. But for all of us there was the knowledge that a song could be about things other than love, kissing, and having a nice dance."

While the surly and smart Simonon attended art school, the more flamboyant and cocksure Jones made his first forays into music with his short-lived band London SS, which featured future Damned and Generation X founder members Rat Scabies and Tony James. The band lasted barely a year, but during that time there were important pointers to the future - among the musicians who auditioned were Jones's pal Simonon and drummer Terry Chimes.

One day, while they signing on for their dole money, Jones and Simonon spotted a face they recognised from the around London scene - John Mellor, better known by his more proletarian-sounding nickname Joe Strummer. Born the son of diplomat in 1952 and privately educated, Strummer's background may have been very different from the two stone-faced proto-punks staring back at him, but his love of music and desire to do something - anything - with his life was much the same. After a stint as a Dylan-and-Guthrie-inspired folk singer called Woody Mellor, Strummer was living in a squat and fronting the respected pub-rock band The 101ers, who both Simonon and Jones had seen and enjoyed. They had been particularly impressed by the front man's energetic performance and aggressive rhythm-guitar playing.

They were encouraged by the man who would eventually become their manager, the charismatic Bernie Rhodes. Rhodes was a friend of Jones and not only was he ambitious, he was also intent on instilling his own political and cultural agendas into a band. Rhodes had already unwittingly played a major part in punk history by introducing John Lydon to the rest of the members of the Sex Pistols. Paul and Mick contacted Strummer to join the new outfit they were putting together. All involved had already been to see - and been blow away - by the Sex Pistols, a group of North and West London contemporaries, and it was at a Pistols show in May 1976 that Strummer was first formally approached. After a day's thought, and swayed by their ambition, mischievousness, and shared hatred of the lame rock bands of the day, Strummer was in.

Virtually camping at Rhodes's Rehearsal Rehearsals in Camden Market stables, the trio began writing songs and refining a sound, a look, an approach, and an attitude. The two songwriters, Strummer and Jones, each took guitar and vocal duties. Their differing singing and playing styles complemented one another perfectly; Jones had a gentler, higher singing voice and a fluid guitar-playing style, while Strummer compensated for his lack of natural melody with distinctive, raw vocals and a stabbing, rhythmic approach to his instrument that would be a huge influence on punk.

Simonon, meanwhile, took up the easier-to-handle role of bass guitarist. Though he was only mastering the basics, with his chiselled film-star looks and natural sartorial style, he looked cooler than either Jones or Strummer, and was once described as "the most handsome man in London". Also joining this early line-up was another guitarist, Keith Levene, who was a valuable musical foil to Strummer's rudimentary rhythm guitar.

Settling on the name The Clash (Simonon's choice, after noticing the word repeatedly appearing in a copy of the Evening Standard), they went in search of a drummer and settled on Terry Chimes, later credited on albums as 'Tory Crimes'.

after some intense rehearsal the five-piece group travelled to Sheffield to play their first show at the Black Swan pub in July 1976. During the following month, Levene was unceremoniously ejected from the band; it was, apparently, a (ahem) clash of personality with Jones that was the reason for Levene's departure.

Levene would soon resurface in 1978, alongside John Lydon, who had dropped the 'Rotten' epithet, in Public Image Limited, whose post-punk output would be as musically influential as that of the Pistols, and more commercially successful, too. Ironically, it was a partnership which began during The Clash's debut performance, Levene's memories of which offer a telling insight into the earliest days of a band, who at that point didn't always present a united front.

"The first time I spoke to John about doing something," Levene told me in 2003, "was when The Clash supported the Pistols in Sheffield, but I actually knew him beforehand through John Beverley, who I played in the Flowers Of Romance with, and who as Sid Vicious went on to join John's band. So we were both sitting on our own, and I thought, fuck it, I'll go and talk to him because he looked so fucking pissed off. We both hated our respective bands. I knew I definitely wanted to leave The Clash and John and I had already spoken about getting together if we did. But I don't think he believed I would actually leave them". So did he jump or was he pushed?

As Levene noted, the force behind everything was manager Bernie Rhodes. Like the Pistols' manager, Malcolm McLaren, Rhodes was an ideas-man, a natural agitator, restless and opinionated. Rhodes was intent on applying his radical ideas to the rock 'n' roll format, and it worked. During one of their early TV interviews, Joe Strummer directed the camera towards Rhodes and declared, "This is the man who invented punk."

"You have to understand that Bernie Rhodes was absolutely integral to the birth of The Clash," Simonon agreed when I questioned him over a quarter of a century later. "After rehearsals we'd sit down and ask each other what we wanted out of it, and there's that famous line about Terry Chimes replying 'I want a Lamborghini', which was fine for him. But, yeah, we cross-referenced with each other and asked, 'Where are we going? What makes this band different?' rather than, 'Let's all get drunk, pull birds, and play guitars', and that's it. We wanted more depth, a more human approach..."

As 1977 dawned, The Clash found themselves perfectly placed and began to speak of a 'year zero' approach to music that wiped the slate clean and only looked to the future. The Sex Pistols had already galvanised a new movement that drew together art students, small groups of alienated middle-class kids from the suburbs, and working-class kids from the different neighbourhoods of London. The Clash played with the Pistols as well as such other new bands as the Damned and the ace, all-girl trio the Slits.

All these bands were united by having only a basic grasp of their instruments and a healthy disdain for all that had gone before. "No Elvis, Beatles, or Rolling Stones in 1977," spat Strummer, and he meant it. As they got more and more gigs under their belts, the word began to seep out, eventually reaching NME, Melody Maker, and Record Mirror, who began to fill more column inches with talk of this new, exciting movement. 'Punk' passed into the parlance of young music fans and the record companies, never slow to spot a trend that might lead to turning a buck,

began to take an interest.

There was no doubt that, along with the Pistols, The Clash were certainly the most fascinating of the new breed. Though there was a certain raw shoddiness to their early sound, a complete dedication to their art - including, at various times, living in their rehearsal room - quickly honed them into a tight and thrilling live band. The songs also had a strong socio-political left-wing message, while their paint-splattered, Pollock-inspired clothes (created by Simonon) offered a look that was hard-edged, new, and a much-needed antidote to their looser-looking contemporaries, most of whom were still dressing like it was the 60s. To hammer the point home, they also daubed slogans onto their instruments and street-and-stage clothes (for they were one and the same), such as 'Creative Violence' and their retort to the 60s mantra of 'Love & Peace': 'Hate & War'. Strummer further outlined the band's ethos in an early piece, stating, "I think people ought to know that we're anti-Fascist, we're anti-violence, we're anti-racist, and we're pro-creative. We're against ignorance."

The first wave of UK punk coincided with the infamous Anarchy tour of December 1976 in which The Clash, the Sex Pistols and the Damned hit the road with ex-New York Doll guitarist Johnny Thunders's Heartbreakers, a piratical but likeable band often acknowledged as being the first to introduce heroin into the British punk scene. The four bands shared first a tour bus and many drunken shenanigans, and then collective disbelief, as shows were cancelled following the Pistols' infamous 'Bill Grundy Incident' - their expletive-riddled debut TV appearance on Thames Television's 'Today' show . Overnight, punk went national and it was a gift to the reactionary UK tabloid newspapers, which lost no time in condemning punk and all it stood for. Thereafter, a wave of negativity washed over the tour which resulted in only seven of the original twenty-one shows going ahead.

1977 was the year that The Clash - and punk - broke big. On January 27, only months into their career, the Clash signed with CBS for an advance of £100,000. Suddenly, the band, who were used to sleeping in draughty squats and existing on lager and speed, had some money to spend. In keeping with the breathtaking speed of events, they recorded their debut album quickly over three weekend

sessions in February 1977 at a cost of just £4000. The iconic cover shot showed Strummer, Jones and Simonon - blank eyed, lean and mean - but not Chimes, whose days with the band were numbered. The album was called simply 'The Clash' and it was preceded by the release of their debut single, 'White Riot', a gritty, high-speed burst of noise which took as its subject the race riots between young black youths and the Metropolitan police that Strummer and Simonon had witnessed at the previous summer's Notting Hill carnival.

In April, the album was released to great critical acclaim. An exercise in economy combined with raw energy, it distilled the

essence of the band in a set of exciting, snarling rock 'n' roll songs. Its themes explored alienation, boredom, frustration, drugs, unemployment, and identity crisis. The song titles alone heavily contributed to the new lexicon and look of punk: 'I'm So Bored With The USA', 'What's My Name', 'Deny', 'Cheat', and 'London's Burning'. A gutsy rendition of Junior Murvin's recent reggae hit 'Police & Thieves' lent further potency to the album and gave a hint of things to come. This perfectly packaged punk cocktail entered the UK album charts at a creditable Number 12, and The Clash had announced themselves as a serious concern.

Meanwhile, after auditioning over 200 drummers to replace the departed Chimes, the trio found a new secret weapon: 21-year-old Nicky 'Topper' Headon, a talented and already experienced rock drummer who was also skilled in jazz, funk, and soul. If, as the saying goes, a band is only as good as its drummer, Topper provided both the solid backbone and the musical diversity necessary to push the quartet forward, and he would be a major contributing factor to their output during the early 80s.

The classic Clash line-up was now in place and the band set out on tour as punk rock snowballed around them. A series of key events took place throughout 1977 that would place punk and The Clash in the history books. These were Queen Elizabeth II's Silver Jubilee celebrations (soundtracked by the Pistols' 'God Save The Queen'), the headline 'White Riot' tour (with the Buzzcocks, Subway Sect and the Slits in support), and a riotous sold-out show at the prestigious Rainbow Theatre, working with legendary dub producer Lee 'Scratch' Perry.

The gigs played during this period were some of the most exciting that provincial Britain had ever witnessed, and the direct influence of The Clash was evident in the many second-wave bands that were soon forming across the UK as a direct result of seeing them; bands such as the Undertones, the Skids, the Ruts, and countless others. For better or for worse, each took their own influence from The Clash. For example, London's Sham 69 took the rough-edged 'man in the street' approach to new extremes, while the Two Tone Records scene led by the Specials, who toured with The Clash, would draw largely on the reggae-ska-punk hybrid that Strummer and Co had pioneered.

The reputation of The Clash and their credibility with the press and young fans alike grew apace; so did the notoriety, helped by mischievous tales of textbook rock 'n' roll tomfoolery. For example, Paul and Topper were arrested as suspected IRA terrorists by the Flying Squad when they were shooting at pigeons from the Rehearsal's rooftop. (The police thought they were firing at passing trains; they were eventually ordered to pay £700 damages to the pigeons' owner). On another occasion they were banned from a hotel chain for the theft of a pillow case, and they survived minor drug busts, increasingly riotous shows, and their fair share of hedonism.

With both band and label keen to capitalise, Strummer and Jones flew to Kingston, Jamaica for a week of song writing. Ripped off by dealers at the docks and fearing for their safety, it wasn't quite the dream trip to their spiritual home they had imagined it would be. The duo spent much of the week in their hotel room, writing such new songs as 'Safe European Home', about their feelings of displacement as Europeans in a foreign land, and the machine-gun rhythms of the powerful, soon-to-be live-favourite 'Tommy Gun'.

The result of this frantic burst of song writing was The Clash's second album, Give 'Em Enough Rope, recorded with Blue Oyster Cult's Sandy Pearlman, an American producer brought in to polish their rough sound into something more accessible for the international market. It worked. The album was a collection of songs that blended tales of robbery, stabbings, and drug raids with more emotive moments, like the tender 'Stay Free'. Neither the raw, amphetamine-fuelled punk of the previous year nor the pan-international flavoured releases that followed it, 'Give 'em Enough Rope' was a fine rock album that has stood the test of time.

It was the first - and maybe the only - true concession the band made towards their record company, who were intent on breaking them in the US and beyond. Indeed, Give 'Em Enough Rope was the band's first release stateside. A reworked version of The Clash was released in America only after their second proper album had introduced them to a nation whose knowledge of UK punk was limited to images of the kamikaze nihilism of Sid Vicious.

Give 'Em Enough Rope was also the first suggestion that The Clash were not part of a short-lived scene, and that they might just be in for the long haul. By the time of the album's release in November 1978, punk had changed irrevocably. Those second-wave bands had turned it into a fixed, easily identifiable subculture. It was no longer in the hands of a select few dozen artistically-minded pioneers mixing vastly different music in London and Manchester, and it was rapidly passing into parody. Just compare Siouxsie And The Banshees with the Buzzcocks or the Subway Sect to see how diverse early punk could be.

Blame for this can partly be laid at the door of the Sex Pistols, who burned bright and then burned out. The level of pressure on the band had merely increased throughout 1977 and was unsustainable, particularly given the inexperience of the band's members. Stir drugs, violence, money wrangles, paranoia, a politicised manager and worldwide fame into the mix and the Pistols were always destined to implode. It happened during their first US tour, a jaunt that ill-advisedly included the less tolerant cowboy towns of the South, where four malnourished London kids faced down audiences composed of burly cowboys who not only didn't understand

them but also saw them as a threat. Their problems were compounded by the slightly sad figure of Sid Vicious, who had gone from goofy young Pistols friend and fan to premier punk player in just 18 months. It was an astonishing rise, but one fuelled by heroin and speed which took his antics to ever dangerous extremes.

Sex Pistols split in January 1978 amid acrimony and exhaustion after a chaotic show in San Francisco, and Vicious continued on a downward spiral aided by drugs and errant girlfriend Nancy Spungen. His fall was even more rapid than his rise, one which culminated in Nancy dying from a stab wound in a hotel room in New York. Accounts of what actually happened that fateful night are still the cause of much debate, but the outcome was a smacked-out Vicious being arrested by the NYPD for his girlfriend's murder and sent to the notoriously tough Rikers Island jail. No one would ever find out the truth, because Sid overdosed on heroin while out on bail in January 1979. Punk had destroyed one of its premier exponents, and in some ways the unwitting Vicious had killed off punk. What once was fun, mischievous, creative, and culturally relevant was now something altogether darker.

The demise of the Pistols was important to understanding the longevity of The Clash because, simply put, it could have been them. The sad end of the band that had kicked down the doors provided a valuable lesson to The Clash. It's also worth

noting, though, that whereas the Sex Pistols were finally revealed to have been motivated by money and McLaren's rampant ego, The Clash were always more concerned with the music and the politics. The punk posturing came second.

Punk had turned remarkably ugly, and disgusted by what they saw, The Clash began to pull further away. It was this conscious decision to diversify, progress, and push on musically that would be evident on their new record. It was an album that is still considered their finest moment, and a rock 'n' roll benchmark today: London Calling.

The **key factor** in the success of The Clash's third album was the US tour that preceded it. Whereas the Pistols had viewed America with **distaste and disgust**, the members of The Clash were far more enamoured of **US culture** and actively embraced it. Movies, 50s rock 'n' roll, outlaw country music, rap, even American clothes and food all had a **huge influence** on the quartet. **The open road** was not something to be tolerated, but to be treated as a portal to a world beyond the confines of Britain and mainland Europe. They approached the tour as a combination of a **cultural fact-finding** mission and a **military invasion.**

In January 1979, while the UK press adopted a told-you-so attitude over the death of Sid Vicious, The Clash left the country for the US tour which, despite a lack of financial support from CBS, was deemed a success. In support was legendry blues rocker Bo Diddley, who opened the show at the band's insistence.

At this point, Bernie Rhodes and the band had fallen out, leaving Melody Maker journalist and Paul's then-girlfriend Caroline Coon to oversee their day-to-day management and The Clash returned to the UK to find not only their finances, but also the punk scene in disarray. Their response was to close ranks and hunker down, putting all they had seen and done into a new set of songs whose sound was broader and which offered more considered political insights which reflected their view of contemporary world events.

The result was a furious and fertile writing session in an anonymous rehearsal room out the back of a car repairs garage just off the Vauxhall Bridge Road in Pimlico. Here, away from the club scene and fortified only by strong weed and McDonald's takeaway, day after day the quartet wrote voraciously. Song after song began to pile up and those songs show a band approaching a creative peak. The quartet worked almost daily from April to August 1979, breaking only for games of football or to retire to a local café for egg and chips (McDonald's aside, they were largely vegetarians). It was a true workman-like approach in more ways than one.

"All ideas came from the group itself, which was why we were such a tight unit in that respect," said Simonon. "This was especially true during London Calling, because we'd parted with Bernie and left our rehearsal studio in Camden because it belonged to him. The Pistols had split up, Sid had died, and we felt quite alone in some ways. But we found the place in Pimlico and became even tighter. In this type of environment you get so tight, to the point where you didn't even need to talk when you were playing; there was a natural communication there."

It was a productive time and the band accrued a stockpile of strong, diverse songs, ranging from the ska of 'Rudie Can't Fail' through the Spector-inspired 'The Card Cheat' to the album's centrepiece title track, and much more besides.

From the rehearsal room, the band hit the studio with producer Guy Stevens. Stevens was an eccentric from the old-school of production. He had worked with Mick Jones's favourites Mott The Hoople, but his eccentric methods and insatiable appetite for booze and pills had meant he'd fallen out of favour with the record labels, who considered him unreliable. Undeterred, Strummer tracked him down to a pub, enlisted his services, and the band relocated to London's Wessex Studios.

"Really, it was Guy's injection of a live energy and enthusiasm that was contagious," Simonon reported. "The thing about London Calling is that it has a quality of the band playing live then and there, which comes down to Guy Stevens."

Video footage later unearthed and made public backs up the claims that Stevens was simultaneously inspired and unhinged. The music the band was recording included a Jamaican ska song set in London, an English rock song about Spanish anarchists, old American rockabilly, and so on. Whichever way anyone looked at it, they were leaving punk behind.

"Writing about what's on your doorstep was always a big thing with The Clash," noted Simonon, "but after a while we had become grown men, certainly by London Calling, and having travelled, we had become more worldly and our thoughts more international, as opposed to being 18-19 years and getting the group to sing about 'Career Opportunities' or 'Garageland'. We'd moved on."

While the band were entering a peak creative period, things behind the scenes were less solid. They were £50,000 in debt, partially because of their refusal to follow the tried and tested routes that other bands followed. They insisted on low ticket prices and famously refused to appear on Top Of The Pops. Furthermore,

to their consternation, they discovered that their record contract turned out to be for 13 albums, rather than the five they'd originally thought.

They began to rectify the situation by employing the service of Blackhill Enterprises, a management and booking agency which had staged some of the major events of the 60s. With Bernie Rhodes out of the picture, Blackhill helped turn the band into a tighter, more professional working-and-touring outfit, and brought a sense of organisation to an otherwise chaotic entity.

Peter Jenner of Blackhill offered an interesting insight into the conflicting characters of the band when he said, "The Clash were this strange mix of personalities. Mick was prone to be moody. Paul was very quiet too. Topper I found a delight. Strummer...I never got hold of what made Joe tick. He had a worldview which I could never work out. As time went on, I don't think he could, either. Joe looked confident, as if he knew all the answers, which I don't know if he actually did...their line was, 'We won't do stadiums, we won't do arenas, and we'll only do small gigs.'" This, incidentally, was a policy that was soon changed.

Blackhill's first move was to send The Clash back to the US for a five-week tour in September 1979. Again, their choice of support acts seemed to echo the diversity of London Calling: Bo Diddley, young country rocker Joe Ely, legendry Stax vocal duo Sam and Dave, and voodoo blues oddity Screamin' Jay Hawkins. For a nation used to their music being compartmentalised - white rock bands on one bill, black blues or soul artists on another - it was surprise, but the fans were generally receptive.

"The crowds were knowledgeable; they knew why the group were putting these guys on," remembered photographer Pennie Smith, who, along with NME cartoonist Ray Lowry in the role of 'war artist', documented the tour with a series of iconic shots. "The whole political side of The Clash - people looked to them as an encyclopaedia. They did a lot of swotting up on everyone's behalf. America had the sense to realise that."

The Clash ended the tour exhausted, malnourished, and homesick, but they had seen the heartland of America first hand. They visited Buddy Holly's grave, kitted themselves in new clothes in Greenwich village (50s rocker shirts, cowboy clothes, biker boots, brothel-creeper shoes, and sharp trousers), and played a series of shows which effectively broke them in America, including an explosive performance at the New York Palladium, where Pennie Smith captured an angular Simonon smashing up his bass in a rare public bout of destruction.

By the time the band returned to the UK, they were agreed that the bass-smashing photo was to be the cover shot of London Calling, and the record was released December 14, 1979. Released as a double album, it was an instant critical and commercial success. A decade later Rolling Stone would famously, and somewhat oddly, vote the album the best of the 1980s. Its lead single was its title track. With such lines as "The ice age is coming, the sun's zooming in/Engines stop running, the wheat is growing thin," the tone of London Calling seemed to suggest a world in economic conflict and environmental decline.

"We saw a map that showed what would happen if the Thames barrier flooded," Mick Jones explained. "Where we lived would be under water. That's what the song is about. Joe wrote the lyrics in a taxi going along the river."

Elsewhere, though, the album was far more upbeat, and read like a rough guide to over 30 years of rock 'n' roll. There were criticisms, however, and these were generally points well made; the NME pointed out Joe and Mick's inability to write credible songs about male-female relationships and their penchant for machismo and self-mythologizing. Perhaps they failed to appreciate that it was these very qualities that were winning the band its rapidly expanding fan base.

With minimal TV and radio support, the single 'London Calling' reached number 11 in the charts, while the album charted at number nine. It also entered the US Billboard chart at 27; no mean feat in a market dominated by home-grown artists.

The Clash crowned a glorious year with two intimate and celebratory Christmas shows at Acklam Hall under the Westway, including one on Christmas day which drew a meagre crowd, as few people actually believed that these now bona fide stars would play a small community hall, let alone on Christmas day.

The 70s were over, and though The Clash would go on to greater commercial success, the first year of the next decade would prove to be less kind. They launched into a lengthy UK tour, dubbed the 16 Tonnes tour, in January 1980 and it was then that the first chinks in the hitherto-impenetrable Clash armour began to appear. In Sheffield, a road-weary Jones refused to play an encore of 'White Riot', a song he thought they had outgrown. Strummer reacted by punching his friend full force in the face.

"It was a pivotal moment," road manager and band confidante Johnny Green told author Pat Gilbert in his excellent biography Passion Is A Fashion: The Clash. "He whacked him, there was blood everywhere. Cut lip. Bloody teeth. We bandaged him up...bandana'd him to cover it up."

The band launched into their '77 signature tune, but Jones put his guitar down and walked off halfway though the song. Though the subject was considered closed, this moment can be recognized as the beginning of the end for the Strummer-Jones partnership. By resorting to violence, Strummer, the street poet and people's politico, had revealed himself to be less articulate than his public persona, while Jones's rather petulant actions confirmed to many that he was becoming a prima donna whose mood swings controlled the band's decision-making.

In any event, the machine kept rolling. On a rare day off, the band hit the studio with their support act, a young reggae producer/MC named Mikey Dread, at the controls. They cut a new song, a subterranean-sounding outlaw dub tune called 'Bankrobber', a key song that was, according to Simonon, initially dismissed by CBS executives as sounding "like Bowie played backwards".

"Joe wrote this almost all by himself," said Jones recently. "He got criticised because people knew his father hadn't been a bank robber, as he sang in the song, but the character wasn't meant to be him. The label boss thought we were going in the wrong direction and refused to release it for ages. He came to the airport once as we were checking our bags in, and stood arguing with us. When they finally put it out it was one of our biggest records."

March saw the release of Rude Boy, a film about a young Clash fan-cum-roadie, played by inexperienced actor and fan Ray Range and set against the racially-unstable backdrop of the early Thatcher years. Though the band had appeared half-acting in a number of scenes, and the film itself was built around some amazing live footage, they quickly distanced themselves from it. Although the film was far from accomplished, it did give a valuable insight into the morally and musically confused mindset of punk as it entered a new decade, and is essential viewing for any Clash fans today.

Meanwhile, they again toured the US, followed by a trip to Kingston, Jamaica to record some reggae songs at Channel One studios in the ghetto and then on to the Power Station in Manhattan. Any tensions between Jones and Strummer were buried as they busied themselves writing a new set of songs in a frantic burst, as was becoming customary. This time, though, they were aided and abetted by a number of musician friends, including Mikey Dread, Strummer's pal from The 101ers Tymon Dogg, Norman Watt-Roy and Mick Gallagher of The Blockheads, and Jones's then-girlfriend Ellen Foley, a backing singer for Meatloaf.

Though they were busy in the studio creating their ambitious triple-album epic Sandinista, they also soaked up everything the city had to offer, including some emerging rap music, most of it on the Sugarhill label, blasting from street-corner boom-boxes. Mick and Joe wrote 'The Magnificent Seven' and 'Lightning Strikes' in response, becoming the first white British group to incorporate hip-hop. This bold move proved to be highly influential in the cross-pollination of musical genres which later occurred throughout the 80s and into the 90s.

"It was Joe who suggested, 'Why don't we do it like a rap tune?'" Mick Jones said of 'The Magnificent Seven'. "It was another form we mastered. Even though it's a rap, it's still got a tune. It was originally going to be called 'The Magnificent Seven Rap-O-Clappers' because we all did this off-beat clapping in the toilets of Electric Ladyland studios in New York. We did a lot of recording in those toilets! It was the echo in there that was good."

Credit is due to The Clash for sticking to their beliefs that music should be available for everyone, and therefore sold cheaply even if it ate into their own personal profits, which it continuously did. They understood and respected their young fan base. So when the triple-vinyl, 36-song Sandinista! was released in December 1980 for the price of a single album - and a mere 12 months after the release of London Calling - it certainly represented value for money. It wasn't, however, a great record by any stretch of the imagination. Lacking any sense of economy or self-censorship, the quartet threw in the works; rabble-rousing anthems, numerous dub cuts, jazz, calypso, cod-rap (just because they dabbled in rap didn't mean it was all necessarily good), and various other cack-handed styles, and they ended up with 145 minutes of incohesive music. For once, The Clash's prolific work-rate and desire to move continually in new directions may have got the better of them.

"I remember thinking 'Is this some kind of bloated arrogance?'" Strummer said in an interview in 1981. "I could imagine some U.S. group doing it, Styx or Foreigner, all those overblown outfits. But then I figured if we could get it for the same price as one [album], more power to us."

Pennie Smith's cover for Sandinista! captured the band, fresh from a Don Letts-directed video shoot for its lead single, 'The Call Up', in military clothes beneath a bridge in North London. As with the music within, even the cover shot seemed somehow less striking or evocative than those of the previous three albums. Much of the influential British music press were of the same opinion, and Sandinista! was largely panned, although it entered the UK charts at number 19. Its second single, 'Hitsville UK', peaked at a career low of 56. As they entered 1981, The Clash became fully aware of the fickle nature of musical taste and suspected that they may have blown it.

In times of adversity, The Clash had a clear tendency either to close ranks or reshuffle their organisation. This they did by re-hiring firebrand manager Bernie Rhodes, whose anarchic energy they felt was missing from their more streamlined recent operations. Incredibly, after five years The Clash were, at least as a collective, in their worst financial position ever.

"They were £500,000 in debt," a magnanimous Rhodes told biographer Pat Gilbert in 1999. "I had to dig them out of a hole...to use a classic car analogy, the Clash was a rusty wreck and I had to do it up and put my updated engine back in there."

all was not lost. Sandinista! climbed to a higher position in the much bigger U.S. market than London Calling had, and it retailed there at a premium price, Clearly, those fabled ethics didn't stretch across salt water. Their U.S. label, however, scrapped a proposed 60-date American tour.

Britain was rocked by riots in the multi-racial London enclaves of Southall and Brixton during 1981 and the Two-Tone ska scene so influenced by The Clash played as a soundtrack to the social unrest, most notably The Specials' eerie chart-topping single 'Ghost Town'. Leaving the chaos in the UK behind them, the Clash began a tour of Europe. The tour was a warm-up to what many consider to be one of their greatest achievements, a 10-night residency at the 4,000-capacity Bond's International Casino on the sleazy periphery of a pre-Rudy-Giuliani Times Square in New York.

The first show went ahead as planned, but afterwards fire officials intervened and deemed the shows a fire risk, reducing the capacity to a mere 1,750 fans per night. To compensate, the venue cancelled bookings with Gary Glitter and The Stranglers and increased The Clash's run to 16 shows, with some extra day-time matinees.

Nevertheless, many of the fans who showed for the next day's afternoon show found themselves turned away. They reacted by going on a rampage. It was a mini-riot, captured on film by Don Letts. It prompted the New York Times to run the cover headline "'CLASH' IN TIMES SQUARE". This logistical nightmare turned out to be a PR dream, and the band quickly printed some T-shirts immortalizing the article. New York's black radio stations also began offering heavy airplay for 'The Magnificent Seven'/'The Magnificent Dance'

"We recorded it in both New York and London," Mick Jones told The Sun newspaper in December 2006. "The A and B-sides are the same song, but with two completely different sets of lyrics and some slight musical differences. The idea of the 12-inch was to go further and further out, and to dissemble it. It sounds bitty. We tried to do too much."

Nevertheless, it found favour, first with receptive New Yorkers and then nationally. With support coming from graffiti-artist-turned-MC Futura 2000 and leading hip-hop lights Grandmaster Flash And The Furious Five, the shows were a resounding cross-musical success, and the band affirmed themselves as pioneers. Famous faces rumoured to have been at the Bond's shows included Robert De Niro, Martin Scorsese (whose movie King Of Comedy featured a fleeting cameo from The Clash as street hoodlums), the future Beastie Boys, and John Lydon, who was then living and working in New York with Public Image Limited.

"They were the first band to really embrace that cross-cultural revolution" said producer Rick Rubin, who was also in attendance. "They brought reggae to rock fans. In America everybody loves reggae because of The Clash."

The summer of 1981 saw a UK tour of smaller towns, including Wolverhampton, Preston, Luton, and Reading, a far cry from a two-and-a-half-week stand on Broadway. It was a transitional period for the band, during which old problems began to re-surface. Topper's gargantuan heroin use began to affect his playing and led to overdose scares and run-ins with dealers. On the commercial front, the relative failure of Sandinista! in the UK, combined with the long periods in the US, saw the record-buying public, as well as the critics, in their own country turn their backs on the band.

The British punk scene had also entered its second phase. The initial explosion of five years earlier had long since gone and a new wave of bands had emerged, taking only the negative elements of punk - musical inability, ugliness and violence - and, unlike The Clash, sticking by a refusal to evolve. Bands such as GBH, Discharge, and The Exploited were turning punk into a postcard parody of something once based on creativity, irreverence, and artistic-political intent, while the working class Oi! scene also drew in a malevolent right-wing element. In the States, punk was giving way to the commercial new-wave bands who would reign over MTV (launched that year) and, in the underground, the more extreme sounds of hardcore bands such as Black Flag, Minor Threat, and Dead Kennedys.

The Clash kept plugging away, by this time more an archetypal mainstream rock n' roll band than ever. Whatever their faults, they never included inertia and inactivity. Planning to record a new album cheaply and quickly, they hit a London studio with Who producer Glyn Johns and recorded such strong new songs as Jones's 'Should I Stay Or Should I Go' and Strummer's 'Know Your Rights'. Two of their best songs since the 70s, they were a reassertion of their song-writing skills despite the behind-the-scenes chaos, addictions and doubts that continued to permeate their organization.

Their new album went by the working title of Rat Patrol From Fort Bragg, a reference to the HQ of the US Army's Special Operations Command. Though they didn't know it, it was to be the final album with their classic line-up. They later changed the title to the more hard-hitting and self-explanatory Combat Rock and it heralded a return to the upper reaches of the UK charts.

Upon its release in May 1982 Combat Rock peaked at number two and stayed in the charts for six months. In the US it reached number seven and lingered in the charts for a year. Against the odds, The Clash had enjoyed a spectacular resurrection and the album proved to be their biggest seller.

Despite the years of legwork in clubs and a veritable arsenal of punk anthems, in America The Clash had become arguably more famous as a hip, crossover-rock band than the political punks they were back home.

This was a perception that was confirmed when The Clash were invited to support The Who at baseball's Shea Stadium in Queens, New York, the venue that saw the incredible 'Beatlemania' shows. The Who's most-sussed member, Pete

Townshend, was a big fan who had jammed with The Clash on stage, and he saw the band as the natural heir to The Who's generation-gap-inspired mod explosion of the 60s. Like it or not, The Clash were now part of the rock establishment, receiving rapturous receptions in the types of venues they said they would never play.

The Clash's new-found lofty status was confirmed by the success of their new single, 'Rock The Casbah', which mixed funk and disco to telling effect, and was arguably a struggling Topper Headon's last great contribution to the band.

"It's about the banning of rock 'n' roll in Iran," Mick Jones said in December 2006. "This was written almost entirely in the studio in New York by Topper Headon, his finest hour. It was a huge international hit. The Falklands War was happening then, which was affecting us. We changed [the album title] because of the war."

Despite its commercial success, Combat Rock was not without its faults. It was an uneven, inconsistent collection that many loyal fans saw as a commercialisation of their own style and ideas - in other words, a sell-out. In some ways they were right. The truth was that The Clash's cornerstone song-writing partnership of Jones and Strummer had been pulling in two clearly different directions. Jones wanted to play the arenas like The Who had, while man-of-the-people Strummer wanted to experiment, delve further into black music, and forge forward in ever new directions.

With many other resentments and niggles rising to the surface after six hectic years of hard toil, and Headon's heroin dependency getting worse and worse, something had to give. In the end it was Mick Jones, the man who gave the band their melody, their stubbornness, and their guitar-hero flair, who was dismissed. It happened around the time of the Notting Hill Carnival of 1983. According to the rest of the band, Mick had become aloof, uncommunicative, and prone to not turning up for rehearsals. Spurred on by Bernie Rhodes, Strummer confronted Jones and asked him to leave one afternoon at Camden's Rehearsal Rehearsals, mere yards from where the band had come together seven years earlier. Simonon awkwardly backed him up.

"Me and Joe had been talking about it, and it got to the point where I said, 'We're grown men, I can't take any more of this, and Joe agreed," a wistful Paul told Mojo in 1999. "We were both in agreement that we were fed up, we wanted to get on with the job, rather than waiting around for Mick. Mick said to me 'What do you say?' and I said 'Well, yeah...' I think he felt let down by that."

If legend is to believed, after his sacking Jones went home, made a series of phone calls and effectively put together a new band by the end of the day.

Initially called TRAC, they would eventually evolve into Big Audio Dynamite and enjoy a healthy career throughout the rest of the decade.

The band had broken America, but America, or rather the relentless cycle of touring, recording and more than their fair share of partying, had also broken them. The Clash as everyone knew them were effectively over.

Being the dogged individuals they were, however, Strummer and Simonon bravely and probably unwisely carried on, reasoning that The Clash was bigger than any of its individual members. They were unfortunately proven wrong.

The line-up that recorded and released the **final Clash album** in 1985 was **barely recognisable** to fans, critics, and associates alike. The prophetically-titled Cut The Crap contained a collection of **shabby songs** that had strayed so far from what made the band great in the first place that they would never be able to return.

The problem was two-fold. The musical landscape had changed and The Clash had mistakenly tried to follow it, creating music that relied heavily on synthesisers and soulless drum machine rhythms that gave the band a flat, robotic sound especially when compared to the powerhouse style of Topper Headen. The second problem was that despite Strummer's best efforts, The Clash themselves were barely recognisable, their line-up padded out by three members who were seen as little more than hired hands.

Young guitarists Nick Sheppard (formerly of Bristol band The Cortinas) and Vince White and drummer Pete Howard were the new members with considerable shoes to fill. Perhaps if this final Clash line-up had made a strong album, it wouldn't have mattered, but though Cut The Crap painted a realistic picture of life in Thatcher's Britain, it clearly lacked the ideas, diversity, and inspired anger of the band's earlier work.

The tour that accompanied the album also involved a radical re-think. Instead of the lean, mean touring machine of an all-for-one last gang in town that fans were used to, the band opted to go back to basics by undertaking a busking tour of town centres, the band members travelling separately and adhering to a set of rules that deemed each member would take with them £10, their instruments and a change of underwear. Though the tour continued The Clash's everyman tradition of allowing band and fans to engage on the same level, the spark was somehow gone.

With both Cut The Crap and the accompanying single 'This Is England' being critically panned, this last gasp of a great band is now acknowledged as little more than a footnote to the history of a band which really ended when Mick Jones walked out of the door. After a show in Athens in 1985, Strummer fled to Spain and effectively broke up the band. They would never perform again.

It had been a busy ten years.

In the wake of The Clash, the band members embarked on a variety of projects. Paul Simonon released a **Latino-influenced** album with Havana 3am before giving up music to return to his first love of painting. Today he remains a respected and successful visual artist. He returned to music in 2006 when he joined **Damon Albarn**'s new project The Good, The Bad & The Queen, who at the time of writing are bathing in the glow of a **critically acclaimed** and commercially successful album. Mick

Jones, meanwhile, launched **Big Audio Dynamite** (aka B.A.D.) which existed in various forms from 1984 to 1998 and released a series of **albums and singles**, most notably the #11 hit single 'E=MC2'. It was Jones's work as a producer that introduced The Clash's most musically **talented songwriter** to a **new generation** when he produced the two albums by The Libertines, a band seen by some as the **natural heirs** to The Clash's considerable crown, and Down In Albion, the album by **Pete Doherty**'s post-Libertines band, Babyshambles. Jones also formed Carbon/Silicon with his childhood friend Tony James, which continues to perform and release music, largely in **MP3** format.

The post-Clash years were less kind to Topper Headon, who struggled with heroin addiction and failed to match past glories. Joe Strummer immersed himself in the movie world, appearing in a number of films and writing soundtracks, as well as performing with The Pogues. He returned in the 90s with Joe Strummer & The Mescaleros, who released a series of strong albums that recalled the wide musical outlook of London Calling and which found favour with a young generation of fans, many of whom discovered The Clash via contemporary punk bands such as Green Day and Rancid.

Ironically, The Clash enjoyed their biggest hit when their single 'Should I Stay Or Should I Go' was used on a Levi's advertising campaign and went straight to number one in the UK singles charts upon its release in 1991. Despite the commercial re-birth, critics and many long-standing fans were quick to point out that the band renting out their music to advertise jeans smacked of hypocrisy.

Though rumours continually circulated in the music press about the possibility of the Clash reforming - not least when a flabby Sex Pistols re-emerged in 1996 - the band's members remained tight-lipped and non-committal.

Strummer and Jones came together in performance one more time in November 2002 when the guitarist joined the frontman on stage back on their home turf of West London at a benefit show for striking city firemen. They had come full circle, all past problems and disputes forgotten, Strummer and Jones were united by music and politics once again. Nobody could have imagined that this show was a full stop to the band's career. A few weeks later, Strummer passed away unexpectedly, though peacefully, at his Somerset home on December 22, 2006, aged just 50.

What remains is a legacy as strong as that of any act in the world - a band which continues to sell records and inspire new musicians, both in their sound and their outlook. "To inspire people, even just for one second, is worth something," Simonon said recently. "To be honest, we were blokes with guitars, and it's unlikely we could change the world, but at 18 you at least think it's  possible - and it is, but maybe not in the way you first think. The amount of people who come up and say we changed their lives and gave them a whole different concept of how to look at things is fantastic."

Bibliography

All interviews by Ben Myers unless otherwise stated. Both highly recommended texts for fans of the bands, the two most important primary sources of fact-checking for this piece were Last Gang In Town: The Story Of The Clash by Marcus Gray (Fourth Estate, 1995) and Passion Is A Fashion: The Clash by Pat Gilbert (Aurum Press, 2005). Thanks also to Simon Hargreaves at James Grant and Adelle Stripe.

DiSCOGRAPHY

Author's Note:

The task of compiling a comprehensive discography of The Clash is not an easy one. Since the split, they've achieved almost mythical status and an already substantial catalogue has been bolstered by a steady stream of demos, unreleased tracks, reissues, compilations and hour upon hour of unheard live footage.

While it's surely every collector's dream to continue to discover new gems from such a seminal and influential band, the reality is that there has been much repetition and recycling of staple Clash tunes.

Of course, this does not claim to be the definitive Clash discography, but within it you will find a complete overview of their official recorded output. Where there have been alternative import versions, I have referred to the band's UK discography. In the case of double or triple albums, to retain authenticity I have referred to the original sides, rather than discs. All releases are on Columbia Records.

I have also chosen to rate each song, rather than album, giving each one to five stars; again, not an easy task. Everyone has a favourite Clash song, and this author's changes daily, so these scores are just one lifelong fan's humble opinion and I guarantee you will disagree with certain opinions. Tomorrow, I probably will too, but that, surely, is half the fun of rock 'n' roll?

There is no right and wrong - just the music.

Ben Myers Spring 2007. www.benmyers.com

STuDiO ALBUMS

THE CLASH (April 8, 1977)
'Janie Jones' / 'Remote Control' / 'I'm So Bored With The USA' / 'White Riot' / 'Hate & War' / 'What's My Name?' / 'Deny' / 'London's Burning' / 'Career Opportunities' / 'Cheat' / 'Protex Blue' / 'Police & Thieves' / '48 Hours' / 'Garageland'

'Janie Jones' ***
A skipping drum beat, a burst of guitar, and the gruff sneering lyrics, "He's in love with the rock 'n' roll world", and The Clash had laid out their stall in simplistic, rough-hewn style.

'Remote Control' **
A relatively poppy song by 1977 punk standards, 'Remote Control' contained the

last vestiges of the band's pub-rock roots. The far-from-precise production fails to lift this song beyond being anything more than an early live favourite.

'I'm So Bored With The USA' ****

With American soft rock dominating the airwaves and world politics, The Clash wrote this, a charged diatribe against American cultural imperialism, which dared to suggest, quite brilliantly, that perhaps the US was giving consumers nothing but disposable, worthless rubbish.

'White Riot' *****

Arguably still the definitive Clash song, and certainly one of punk's most enduring, 'White Riot' was famously penned after Strummer and Simonon got caught up in race riots at the Notting Hill Carnival. In just under 120 thrilling seconds you can almost smell the burning cars and feel the breaking of glass underfoot.

'Hate & War' ***

Not quite as abrasive as its easily-stencilled title might suggest, 'Hate & War' was one of the band's earliest songs, but never destined to be a classic. It looked good on their shirts, though.

'What's My Name?' ***

An edgy, boorish, and slightly malevolent slice of adolescence identity crisis, this garage tune helped shaped the psyche of punk; it's confused, alienated, and more than a little pissed off.

'Deny' **

A reasonably straight-forward, mid-paced, rudimentary song with particularly phlegmatic vocals by Joe Strummer, 'Deny' was closer to filler than killer. It was through songs such as this, though, that the seeds of punk were planted outside of London, as the provinces began to rock to similar-sounding songs. Listen to this and think of such second-wave bands as the Skids, Penetration, and the Members.

'London's Burning' ***

Taking inspiration from the nursery rhyme of the same name, 'London's Burning' was another song to set the punk tone with blunt and provocative intent, and showed the capital city to be the birthplace of this new movement: "London's burning with boredom now."

'Career Opportunities' ****

Along with 'White Riot', this song was another sub-two-minute product of The Clash's productive early writing sessions that came with an agenda, in this case, a refusal to buy into empty material gains by working at a job you hate. Lines such as "I hate the civil service rules/I won't open letter bombs for you" were

inspired by real-life experience, in this case Mick Jones's time opening mail for a textbook-tedious governmental subdivision. The music is suitably ragged and forthright.

'Cheat' **

An aggro street-punk song with a basic beat, its lack of a discernible hook meant it got lost somewhat amongst the stronger songs of their debut. A rare FX-laden guitar sound does, however, sear through the raw production, while Mick Jones's simple two-note guitar solo was soon to become something of a trademark. See also 'Tommy Gun'.

'Protex Blue' ***

Another song that recalls the more traditional pub-to-glam rock beginnings of Strummer's 101ers and Jones's London SS, 'Protex Blue' is relatively perky compared to more nihilistic sounding songs on The Clash, almost an update of 50s rock 'n' roll. The subject matter provides a departure, too. The title was inspired by a brand of condom available in the 1970s; hence the declaration of "Johnny! Johnny!" at the song's close.

'Police & Thieves' *****

The importance of a white punk band deftly covering Junior Murvin's recent reggae hit cannot be underestimated. This excellent interpretation, complete with clunking, competing guitars, kicked down musical divisions and directly inspired the entire invention of the Two-Tone ska scene, and, beyond that, modern ska-punk. Bob Marley, for one, responded with 1977's 'Punky Reggae Party'.

'48 Hours' **

'48 Hours' is perhaps of most interest for highlighting the burgeoning vocal partnership of Strummer and Jones - one raw and raspy, the other softer and more melodic. Somehow, though, they worked. This song boisterously blunders its way through in a mere one-and-a-half minutes and sounds in danger of falling apart at any minute. That's no bad thing, though.

'Garageland' ****

'Garageland' was famously inspired by a caustic review of a live performance supporting the Sex Pistols, in which NME's Charles Shaar Murray wrote, "The Clash are the kind of garage band who should be returned to the garage immediately, preferably with the engine running." With a driving beat, an anti-establishment stance, and fleeting moments of tenderness, the response was pure Clash, an aural manifesto by four firebrands ready to prove the critics wrong.

A **US version** of The Clash appeared in 1979 with an alternative tracklisting. As it remains widely available in the UK today and is often mistakenly seen as the band's debut, it is worthy of note. The **tracklisting** for this US version is: 'Clash City Rockers' / 'I'm So Bored With The USA' / 'Remote Control' / 'Complete Control' / 'White Riot' / '(White Man) In Hammersmith Palais' / 'London's Burning' / 'I Fought The Law' / 'Janie Jones' / 'Career Opportunities' / 'What's My Name?' / 'Hate & War' / 'Police & Thieves' / 'Jail Guitar Doors' / 'Garageland'.

GIVE 'EM ENOUGH ROPE
(November 10, 1978)

'Safe European Home' / 'English Civil War' / 'Tommy Gun' / 'Julie's Been Working for the Drug Squad' / 'Last Gang in Town' / 'Guns on the Roof' / 'Drug-Stabbing Time' / 'Stay Free' / 'Cheapskates' / 'All the Young Punks (New Boots and Contracts)'

'Safe European Home' ****

This opener of The Clash's slicker-sounding second album was written by Strummer and Jones on a song-writing trip to Jamaica in which their white, Western sensibilities were quickly illuminated when they were ripped off scoring weed in

Kingston. To their credit, they didn't hide their shortcomings, with lyrics such as "Yes I'd stay and be a tourist but I can't take the gunplay". The opening crack of Topper Headon's snare drum and burst of guitars still sounds like an air strike today.

'English Civil War' ****

Tightly-wound, strident, and with its lip curled into a snarl, 'English Civil War' was loosely inspired by the American Civil War song, 'When Johnny Comes Marching Home', which a young Strummer had learnt during his school days. Within it, The Clash indirectly warn of impending conflict within Britain, taken by many listeners to be a commentary on the rise of the National Front-led far right in the late 70s.

'Tommy Gun' ****

From the opening rat-a-tat gun-fire beat through to its dramatic conclusion, 'Tommy Gun' is another key Clash song, the sound of a band hitting an energetic peak. The title, of course, refers to the old-time gangster's gun of choice, but was also the name bestowed upon a martyred soldier, a lyrical message which, read in the context of the early twenty-first century, sounds unnervingly prophetic. Live footage of this song is among some of the band's best.

'Julie's Been Working for the Drug Squad' ***

Piano-led and telling a murky real-life tale of drug busts and police informants, 'Julie's Been Working for the Drug Squad' has an upbeat, bar-room feel to it. It's the band at their poppiest, and clearly evolving into a broader, tighter-sounding proposition. The song was inspired by a recent undercover sting called Operation Julie.

'Last Gang in Town' ***

'Last Gang in Town' can be seen as a critique of the in-fighting amongst rock and pop cultures, cliques, and sub-divisions - mods, rockers, skinheads, and the like. Never shy of romanticising or self mythologising, however, it also seems like a celebration of the quartet's own position as kings of the street punks. It may have been an obvious route to take, but the handle stuck.

'Guns on the Roof' ***

Another true tale, this time concerning the comical arrests of various members of The Clash's camp after they tried to shoot a neighbour's prize pigeons from the rooftop of Rehearsal Rehearsals. Witnesses thought they were shooting at passing trains and the bemused punks were soon faced by the Met police anti-terror squad.

'Drug-Stabbing Time' **

The power of Give 'Em Enough Rope's opening salvo couldn't be maintained over the course of a full album, and 'Drug Stabbing Time', an innocuous-sounding, bluesy, bar-room rock song, felt like a filler. Though a relatively catchy tale of drug debts and deals gone wrong, it sounds like a band trying a little too hard to present themselves as modern urban outlaws.

'Stay Free' *****

Few songs born out of punk have ever been quite as emotive and poignant as 'Stay Free'. A Mick Jones-penned tale based on the rites de passage scrapes of his friend and band associate Robin Crocker that culminated in a stint in Brixton prison, 'Stay Free' is an affectionate and melodic flipside to The Clash's yob-punk songs of the previous year - teary-eyed, but never sentimental, and also brilliant.

'Cheapskates' **

Perhaps the weakest song on the album, 'Cheapskates' is a straight-forward, mid-tempo song the only real purpose of which seems to be furthering the image, lifestyle, and outlook of a socially-aware band, aimed at refuting claims that they're rich rock stars.

'All the Young Punks (New Boots and Contracts)' ***

As British punk was evolving into a definable genre or sub-culture, complete with rules, regulations, and uniforms, The Clash were pulling away, widening their scope, and commenting on the scene they had helped create with songs such this. An anthemic, driven rock song, 'All The Young Punks...' again mythologises the beginnings of the band while also suggesting that newer, younger bands were being quick to jump on punk's bandwagon.

LONDON CALLING (December 14, 1979)

'London Calling' / 'Brand New Cadillac' / 'Jimmy Jazz' / 'Hateful' / 'Rudie Can't Fail' / 'Spanish Bombs' / 'The Right Profile' / 'Lost in the Supermarket' / 'Clampdown' / 'The Guns of Brixton' / 'Wrong 'Em Boyo' / 'Death or Glory' / 'Koka Kola' / 'The Card Cheat' / 'Lover's Rock' / 'Four Horseman' / 'I'm Not Down' / 'Revolution Rock' / 'Train in Vain'

'London Calling' *****

From the jarring guitars of its atmospheric opening, 'London Calling' is a song that is nothing short of iconic. The tone and production perfectly suit the apocalyptical lyrics about a city in decline. Over resonant, chiming chords, in a few short minutes the band manage to comment on the nuclear era and climate while creating a sound track for the city they love, which is presented with warts and all. As album signature songs go, this is up there with the best of them.

'Brand New Cadillac' ***

Originally recorded by Vince Taylor, the English-born and Hollywood-raised pioneer of early rock 'n' roll, this 1959 single recorded with his band The Playboys had been a long-time favourites of The Clash, who turned it into an edgy rockabilly rumble perfectly suited to their new bequiffed, black-clad image. It also suggested that, far from dismissing US culture as they had on their debut album, they were actually rather in awe of it. Footnoote: in the mid-60s, Taylor had an acid-induced breakdown mid-performance, and David Bowie would later cite him as a major influence on his Ziggy Stardust creation.

'Jimmy Jazz' ***

If London Calling was an attempt to present a more international sound for The Clash, then its subsequent success was partly because of album tracks like this agreeable mix of ska, R&B, and rock 'n' roll. Introducing horns and acoustic guitars for the first time, 'Jimmy Jazz' was the laid-back sound of a band locking into new sounds with ease and style.

'Hateful' ***

Disengaging themselves further from punk, 'Hateful' was another song that highlighted The Clash's determination to diversify. An up-tempo, slinky song with the same rhythmic energy of rockabilly, with suitably simplistic lyrics, it was one of their most overtly danceable songs up to that time.

'Rudie Can't Fail' ****

Taking the generic character of the naïve Jamaican country boy Rudie down on his cups in the city, and clearly inspired by Jimmy Cliff's Ivan character in The Harder They Come and giving him a London makeover, this ska song is one of The Clash's best. Reggae-ska horns, a skanking backbeat and a Strummer rap all conspire to tell the optimistic tale of the sharply-attired Rudi. The result was a well-orchestrated song deserving of any party soundtrack.

'Spanish Bombs' ****

The Clash had always been a political band, but 'Spanish Bombs' showed a real lyrical development from the anti-everything stance of '77 to this more well-read, widely-travelled presentation at the close of the decade. Name-checking murdered Republican poet Federico Garcia Lorca and dropping in Spanish phrases, it told the tale of the bloody Spanish Civil War of 1936-1939 in which anarchists fought fascists. It was one of their finest moments, a song whose cultural and historical significance hasn't diminished over time.

'The Right Profile' ***

'The Right Profile' was inspired by a biography of actor Montgomery Clift that Joe Strummer had devoured during the making of London Calling. The Clash translated Clift's colourfully tragic life in old-time Hollywood into a song that sounded like it was straight out of New Orleans, such was the swing in its step. It also sounded like these angry firebrands, more commonly associated with speed and urgency, were kicking back and having fun. Incidentally, The Clash's later live album From Here to Eternity would be named after a Clift movie.

'Lost in the Supermarket' ****

Something of an autobiographical tale, the distinctive hushed singing, the subtle guitar lines, the mixture of the personal and the political in lyrics that comment on the mundane consumerism of everyday life in England - this song has the mark of Mick Jones all over it. Musical restraint in the studio paid off; 'Lost in the Supermarket' provides a big, beating heart within the wider body of work.

'Clampdown' ****

Continuing the album's themes of revolution, rebellion, and resistance, 'Clampdown' is a song that can be read as a diatribe against fascism, with lines such as "You start wearing the blue and brown", referring to SS uniforms, and against an unbalanced, unfair, capitalist system that favours the wealthy minority. Whatever the intent,

'Clampdown' was an air-punching anthem to appease all factions of the expanding Clash fan base. The song would later be covered live by the likes of The Strokes, Rage Against The Machine, and Manic Street Preachers' James Dean Bradfield.

'The Guns of Brixton' *****

Although this was the only Clash song written and sung by ice-cool bassist Paul Simonon, it's also, perhaps ironically, one of their greatest and most enduring. Its genius lies in the much-sampled dub-like bass line, Jones's precision arrangement and unique guitar sound. Again inspired in part by the outlaw chic of Jamaican reggae and dub of The Harder They Come, 'The Guns Of Brixton' foreshadowed the race riots that blighted that area of South London just two years later.

'Wrong 'Em Boyo' ***

This song is another fine slice of dirt-stomping ska. It was partially inspired, or at least makes reference to, the black American murderer-turned-folk-hero Stagger Lee, who was immortalised in literally hundreds of blues songs.

'Death or Glory' ***

A song title to stencil on your leather jacket if ever there was, 'Death Or Glory' is a song about hypocrisy within the punk scene concerning a "gimmick hungry yob...who grabs the mike and tells us he'll die before he's sold". It's a message

summed up brutally and unambiguously in the line "He who fucks nuns will later join the church." Full of righteous ire, The Clash were forging ahead with their own future.

'Koka Kola' **

London Calling is not a perfect album, and with 19 songs it arguably suffers from a lack of editing. This fairly standard-sounding blues-rock song would be a candidate for the cut. Despite this, even the less prominent songs still pose questions and offer wry commentary, in this case concerning the aggressively money-driven advertising world; "Koke adds life where there isn't any", which in today's anti-globalisation climate, continues to ring true. The mis-spelling of 'coke' was presumably to avoid a lawsuit.

'The Card Cheat' ****

Something of an underrated and often overlooked Clash gem, 'The Card Cheat' is grand, refined, and almost Spectoresque in its use of a double-tracked wall-of-sound production and Vegas-era-Elvis-inspired horns. Epic in feel, it tells the hard-bitten tale of a doomed man gambling - seemingly - with cards, and by extension, his life. It's the sound of a band reaching a new level of sophistication; it's hard to believe this was the same band that released 'White Riot' less than three years previously.

'Lover's Rock' **

'Lover's Rock' was easily one of The Clash's most lightweight moments up to that time. As punk was becoming just another subculture, the band almost seemed to be rebelling against that which they had helped to create, and what better way than to write a jaunty, gentle tune, whose title was derived from the emerging innocuous reggae genre of lovesick smooch-pop dubbed 'lover's rock'.

'Four Horseman' ***

A jaunty sounding rock 'n' roll song that sounds like an account of a gang - sound familiar? The song seems to predict the band's forthcoming demise: "They were given all the foods of vanity/And all the instant promises of immortality/But they bit the dust screamin' insanity". Straightforward, but likeable.

'I'm Not Down' **

A descending guitar line and Mike Jones vocal again contributed to a song built upon the same fighting spirit that drove much of their music. Here was a band at ease with melody and intent on making ever more mature music that still carried a message, in this case the survival of The Clash in the face of adversity. Another street fighting song you could dance to, then.

'Revolution Rock' ***

A fine example of how far the band had come, this song pulls together The Clash's love of politics, ska, and new rhythms, adds a horn section, and creates a joyous party song that seems to sum up the album as a whole.

'Train in Vain' ****

It's hard to believe that this song was only added to the album at the very last minute. Written and recorded in 24 hours, it is the Clash at their most mainstream - though that's not a criticism. This lovelorn Jones song exudes emotion and was the first song to break the US Top 30 singles charts; though disputes over releasing such a radio-friendly single were believed to have created disharmony between Jones and Strummer.

SANDINISTA!
(December 12, 1980)

'The Magnificent Seven` / 'Hitsville UK` / 'Junco Partner` / 'Ivan Meets GI Joe` / 'The Leader` / 'Something About England` / 'Rebel Waltz` / 'Look Here` / 'The Crooked Beat` / 'Somebody Got Murdered` / 'One More Time` / 'One More Dub` / 'Lightning Strikes (Not Once But Twice)` / 'Up in Heaven (Not Only Here)` / 'Corner Soul` / 'Let's Go Crazy` / 'If Music Could Talk` / 'The Sound of Sinners` / 'Police on My Back` / 'Midnight Log` / 'The Equaliser` / 'The Call Up`/ 'Washington Bullets` / 'Broadway` / 'Lose This Skin` / 'Charlie Don't Surf` / 'Mensforth Hill` / 'Junkie Slip` / 'Kingston Advice` / 'The Street Parade` / 'Version City` / 'Living in Fame` / 'Silicone on Sapphire` / 'Version Pardner` / 'Career Opportunities` / 'Shepherds Delight`

'The Magnificent Seven' ****

It was not the gritty, urgent punk of their debut or the political world vision of London Calling that broke The Clash in America, but this funk-flavoured, rap-inspired song. The band were always musical magpies quick to appropriate their influences and 'The Magnificent Seven` was inspired by the beats and vocal dynamics of the very earliest artists they had been exposed to in New York. In turn, it became a huge radio hit in the Big Apple, revealing The Clash to be genuine rap-rock pioneers. It's also the only known punk-rap crossover song to name-check philosophers Marx and Engels.

'Hitsville UK' ***

A vast departure for the Clash, the uplifting 'Hitsville UK' is a celebration of the UK's fertile independent record scene, epitomized by the Rough Trade and Factory labels, and almost sounds like a Christmas carol. While its jaunty pop backbeat, spacious production, and use of female vocals, provided by Mick Jones's then-girlfriend Ellen Foley, 'Hitsville UK' recalls prime Motown soul and the overall feel is distinctly seasonal. As a single it was an odd choice, but a surprisingly pleasing one that fitted in perfectly with the early 80s post-punk-pop crossover climate.

'Junco Partner' ***

Of all the reggae excursions upon which the band embarked, in terms of production this is certainly one of the most authentic. 'Junco Partner' dated back to Strummer's pre-Clash tenure with multi-national rock band The 101ers, when the singer picked up the R&B original by James Wayne and incorporated it into the band's set. An early version of the song later resurfaced on The 101ers collection 'Elgin Avenue Breakdown'.

'Ivan Meets GI Joe' ***

Another disco-rock combination inspired by the sounds heard both on the streets and night clubs of New York, 'Ivan Meets GI Joe' deals in a rare Clash commodity: fun. It's also one of many political-leaning songs which is clearly directed towards the USA.

'The Leader' ***

A rockabilly shuffle, 'The Leader' is a simple, strong jam about a corrupt, sexually-obsessed political leader. Though lacking any real meaning, it is nevertheless another highly danceable Clash moment, and given the number of scandals involving Tory MPs during the 80s, it contained a certain kernel of truth.

'Something About England' *

There's something about this song that really grates. Maybe it's Mick Jones's vocals, which seem thin and effeminate even by his standards, or that whatever message Strummer is conveying doesn't translate, or perhaps it's that the song goes for the same epic feel as 'The Card Cheat' but just isn't strong enough. It goes nowhere.

'Rebel Waltz' *

'Rebel Waltz' is a particularly melancholy song for the quartet. Written from the perspective of a soldier, or possibly a revolutionary dissident, the lyrics recall the work of poets such as Lorca, as name checked in 'Spanish Bombs'. Again though, as is true of much of Sandinista!, the ambitious idea is stronger than the execution.

The sound is muddy and the song lacks melody and any colour is washed out to a sepia-hued torpor.

'Look Here' *

This is the point at which it becomes clear to listeners that Sandinista! may have been more fun to write and record than to actually listen to. 'Look Here' is a straight-up boogie-woogie interpretation of legendry jazz pianist Mose Allison's original. All very fine, but from a band that had set itself such lofty standards, it simply didn't cut the mustard.

'The Crooked Beat' **

The keenest member to pursue his love of dub and reggae, and aided throughout Sandinista! by producer/MC Mikey Dread, Paul Simonon sang this song about a South London blues party, the name given to after hours sound system parties. Stripped-down and reverb-laden, the result was a standard dub track and it was hardly groundbreaking.

'Somebody Got Murdered' ****

A clear highlight on a distinctly hit-and-miss collection, 'Somebody Got Murdered' makes up a little for some of the mediocre songs that precede it. The song describes a murder scene, but the overall feeling is not of anger and rage but compassion, as conveyed by Jones's understated whisper and the use of stark, poetic images: "His name cannot be found/A small stain on the pavement/They'll scrub it off the ground."

'One More Time' **

Another Jamaican-inspired dub plate produced by Mikey Dread and with input from Paul Simonon who was clearly advancing and improving as a bassist and a songwriter. Compared to dub titans such as Lee 'Scratch' Perry' and King Tubby, though, 'One More Time' is rather anaemic.

'One More Dub' *

Sandinista! is full of fillers like this instrumental version of 'One More Time'. A worthwhile idea perhaps, but one which should surely have found its was onto the B-side of a single at best. It's a decent tune, but it sounded like a band struggling to justify the decision to release a triple album.

'Lightning Strikes (Not Once But Twice)' **

Recorded at Hendrix's Electric Lady studio in downtown Manhattan in April 1980 during Sandinista!'s earliest sessions, this opening song of Side Three is a valiant attempt at funk. Though Strummer's vocals are clumsy in their urgency, the music is underpinned by some tight funk bass and Topper Headon's drums, and with this The

Clash predated the sound that LA funk-rock quartet Red Hot Chilli Peppers made their own some years later.

"Up in Heaven (Not Only Here)' **

Mick Jones revisited the subject of his tower-block upbringing overlooking the Westway for this jaunty but lightweight rock song. Unlike earlier works, though, it fails to say anything about life in Britain at the dawn of the 80s. A sign, perhaps, that the band were inadvertently watering down the content of their songs?

'Corner Soul' **

More dub vibrations reverberating out of West London, made unique by Strummer.

The band manage to capture some of the party vibes of their beloved Notting Hill Carnival - a shame 'Corner Soul' is not nearly as colourful.

'Let's Go Crazy' **

As if they've stabbed a pin in a map of the world, suddenly the Clash take us to the West Indies for some calypso-pop, complete with steel drums and patois intro/outro. The good intentions pay off and this is a likeable jam, though the results are not vastly different to the type of weak, percussion-laden pop that littered the charts in the early-to-mid 80s.

'If Music Could Talk' *

This isn't good - a jazzy, sax-laden piece of music that wouldn't sound out of place in an overpriced cocktail bar. The only saving grace is that The Clash often pre-dated later musical movements, and this certainly resembles the type of bad, cappuccino-drinking, yuppie jazz-pop of the 80s, thereby at least proving they were always one step ahead of the pack.

'The Sound of Sinners' ***

As if to prove that they really could turn their hand to anything, out of nowhere came a country-gospel tune, full of righteous, God-fearing fervour. Strangely, it works, and 'The Sound of Sinners' is a highly likeable secret buried deep within The Clash's dense body of work. It also bears a similarity to the White Stripes' 2001 breakthrough single 'Hotel Yorba'.

'Police on My Back' ***

This cover of a late-60s minor hit for the Equals is a strong opener for side four of Sandinista! A tale of paranoia, police harassment, and a general state of confusion, The Clash make it their own to such an extent that it wouldn't sound out of place on Give 'Em Enough Rope or London Calling. It's easily one of the album's strongest moments.

'Midnight Log' *

Lyrically this short song tackles the seemingly impenetrable armour of the corporate capitalist world in the bullish us-against-them, black-and-white style synonymous with the band. In a time when rock music was seemingly devoid of protest music, The Clash were asking questions, and sometimes even providing answers. The forgettable, low-key jazzy-rockabilly mélange of sound, however, was a threat to no one.

'The Equaliser' **

Maybe The Clash were testing listeners' patience by shoe-horning more melodicaled dub into an album already suffering from too many meandering, directionless pieces. By stripping things down and piling on the echo-chamber effect, this effort actually surpasses some of Sandinista!'s excursions, but if it had been a single or double album 'The Equaliser' would have no doubt been left on the cutting room floor.

'The Call Up' ***

With the draft still in existence in American society and Vietnam an all too recent memory, The Clash wrote a response about the futility of war. Oddly, 'The Call Up' was the choice for the first single from Sandinista!, odd because though it's an ambitiously arranged mid-tempo funk-punk rock song complete with its 'Devo' synthesizers and jingling bells, it is also devoid of the life breathed into other album tracks. Also note the similarity to Mick Jones's post-Clash band Big Audio Dynamite.

'Washington Bullets' ***

Unlike some of the more laid-back Sandinista! tracks, 'Washington Bullets' is at least focused. It's also one of their most politically astute songs, taking in as it does the Cuban Revolution of 1959, the Nicaraguan Sandinista, the Soviet invasion of Afghanistan, and the Dalai Lama, while articulately criticising US foreign policy. And where the Clash the first punk band to successfully incorporate a xylophone into their sound?

'Broadway' *

Recording in New York, the band were heavily influenced by the streets they walked each night and the cinematic depiction of the city in the recently released movie Taxi Driver. Sadly, unlike the city itself, or the film, this musical homage goes nowhere. Again, the band afforded themselves too much musical freedom.

'Lose This Skin' ***

Just when the listeners are getting acclimatized to Sandinista!, this musical curveball comes along, an overwrought, Celtic-folk-infused, rock jig written by Strummer's busking pal, and later member of his band the Mescaleros, Tymon Dogg. Strangely, it works, not least because of Dogg's distinctly feminine and fragile-sounding vocals, although heard in isolation it sounds like the work of another band entirely.

'Charlie Don't Surf' **

Taking its title from a line bellowed by Robert Duval's gung-ho, surf-obsessed squadron commander Bill Kilgore in Clash favourite Apocalypse Now, there's something about this song that disappoints. Though it seems to these ears to lack a strong, discernible melody, and with pop production that whitewashes the sound, amongst certain hardcore fans this downbeat 50s-flavoured number nevertheless still ranks as a late-career favourite.

'Mensforth Hill' *

'Mensforth Hill' is pure studio experimentation, essentially 'Something About England' played backwards. Perhaps you had to be there, smoking the same stuff as the band. It is self-indulgent, to say the least.

'Junkie Slip' *

'Junkie Slip' is another idea bashed out with little forethought. Little more than a skiffle shuffle with some Strummer ad-libbing added over the top, it sounds like a cack-handed, late night attempt at some impromptu lo-fi funk. In which case, they were successful. But was there any need to release it?

'Kingston Advice' **

Since their visit in 1978, The Clash drew endless inspiration from Jamaica's vibrant capital city. A sprightly rocker with Mick Jones on vocals, 'Kingston Advice' is another, but, once again, it frustratingly goes nowhere. Lyrically, at least, it recalled prime street-level Clash: "In these days see the people run/They have no food but the boy have a gun."

'The Street Parade' **

It's obvious that energy levels dropped and attention began to wander throughout Side Five. Though not a bad typical reggae-rock song, and with the usual precision drum work of Topper Headon, 'The Street Parade' nevertheless is the sound of the bottom of the barrel being scraped.

'Version City' *

Side Six of Sandinista! is the Clash at their most forward-thinking, but it is also largely comprised of recycled ideas and gimmickry, some of which are their weakest to date. 'Version City' sounds like the dominant sounds of the album - reggae, funk, soul, and blues - randomly thrown together.

'Living in Fame' **

After an intro from a plummy-voiced Englishman comes this Mickey Dread-led dub reworking of 'If Music Could Talk'. Dread's vocal, co-writing, and production contribution to The Clash's recorded output is huge, and this is a creditable dub song showcasing his inimitable toasting style. The downside of his appearances was having too many samey laconic-sounding, spliffed-up songs in one place.

'Silicone on Sapphire' **

Here the Clash stumble their way into the 80s. Too much time hanging around NY danceterias may have had a negative effect. Synthesizers, pre-dance music bleeps, and soulless production conspire to remix and reinvent 'Washington Bullets' into an avant garde piece that may have been futuristic at the time but is sadly dated now. An interesting idea, perhaps, but...

'Version Pardner' **

A dub-heavy mix of 'Junco Partner', with the obligatory studio effects, this is another decent dub song in which the influence of Lee 'Scratch' Perry looms large, and is arguably as good as the original.

'Career Opportunities' **

Mickey Gallagher, keyboardist with Ian Dury's band The Blockheads, featured on Sandinista! to such an extent that his sons Ben and Luke Gallagher sang this kiddie-friendly, easy-listening, muzak version of 'Career Opportunities'. There's certainly something endearing about hearing children sing lines like, "They're gonna have to take away my prescription."

'Shepherds Delight' *

In which, 36 songs later, Sandinista!'s batteries finally run out and it's all the band can do to squeeze out this gentle reggae instrumental and which seems almost like an afterthought. The indifference displayed in the song would soon, alas, be echoed by the record-buying public.

COMBAT ROCK (May 14, 1982)

'Know Your Rights' / 'Car Jamming' / 'Should I Stay or Should I Go' / 'Rock the Casbah' / 'Red Angel Dragnet' / 'Straight to Hell' / 'Overpowered by Funk' / 'Atom Tan' / 'Sean Flynn' / 'Ghetto Defendant' / 'Inoculated City' / 'Death is a Star'

'Know Your Rights' ****

"This is a public service announcement - with guitars!" bellows Joe Strummer on this edgy-sounding return to form. Though this lead single stalled at number 43 in the UK charts, it was pure Clash protest, a tense song with choppy guitars that translated live brilliantly. Check out the version on the band's From Here To Eternity 1999 live album for proof.

'Car Jamming' **

The prominent theme on Combat Rock is war and conflict on an international scale. This song tells of a "shy boy from Missouri, boots blown off in a Sixties war", who back home is branded a murderer, a clear reference to Vietnam veterans. Musically, however, it's a straight rock 'n' roll song with a pop bent and sees Mick Jones squeezing some interesting guitar sounds.

'Should I Stay or Should I Go' *****

'London Calling' may be recognised as The Clash's signature tune, but it was this great rock 'n' roll song that remains their biggest hit, albeit when controversially re-released off the back off a Levi's advert ten years later. Timeless and traditional rock 'n' roll, it moves with a swing in its step, drops in Spanish backing vocals courtesy of Strummer, and concerns Mick Jones's indecision to stay in his relationship with girlfriend Ellen Foley. It's a song for which jukeboxes were invented and whose power and subject matter transcends genre and language. It is, quite simply, one of the great modern rock songs.

'Rock the Casbah' *****

Clearly exercising more quality control than on Sandinista!, this excellent disco-funk floor-filler was another latter-day, radio-friendly Clash classic. 'Rock The Casbah' was the creation of Topper Headon, who built a drum loop in the studio and even wrote a set of lyrics which Strummer discarded to replace with a diatribe about the suppression of pop music under extreme religious regimes. It brought in a whole new audience.

'Red Angel Dragnet' **

Soaking up everything New York had to offer, 'Red Angel Dragnet' concerned the killing of Guardian Angel Frankie Melvin, and also once again referenced the film Taxi Driver. While the stripped-down atmosphere funk-rock is agreeably atmospheric, Paul Simonon's Cockney-patois spoken-word vocals are a little brutish and gruff to sit comfortably.

'Straight to Hell' ****

This may well be the last great recorded moment of the band's career, a mini-epic cut down from its original length of seven minutes. It's a truly international-sounding song with a haunting violin backdrop and lots of atmospheric tom-tom work from Topper Headon. Over the top, Strummer sings a spacious song perceived to be about abandoned children fathered by American soldiers in Vietnam. One of the band's most downbeat moments is also one of their best.

'Overpowered by Funk' ***

Just as it says, this is a forceful and muscular funk song. Although Topper was suffering from heroin addiction, his rhythmic influence is stamped all over this album through songs like this American-sounding song, Vietnam and New York being the two main inspirations for the album. Aside from the now-dated synth effects, it's also notable for an appearance from visionary graffiti artist Futura 2000, who also penned the Combat Rock sleeve notes and appeared on stage with the band on a number of occasions.

'Atom Tan' ***

Another song that seems to have been written beneath a mushroom cloud of nuclear-age paranoia, like 'London Calling', 'Atom Tan' sounds too hastily constructed to leave a lasting impression, although its simple rolling riff and Strummer-Jones vocal interplay is still pleasing.

'Sean Flynn' **

Named in honour of Errol Flynn's son, a renowned war photographer who famously rode into battle in Vietnam on his motorbike, 'Sean Flynn' is a near-instrumental which uses flutes to create an Eastern-sounding, almost kabuki-like atmosphere. As a musical experiment, it just about succeeds.

'Ghetto Defendant' ***

'Ghetto Defendant' concerns heroin's effects on inner-city ghettos, and its ability to pacify its users politically. Interestingly, it features an appearance from legendry Beat generation poet Allen Ginsberg, whose spoken-word section named-dropped punk terms like 'slam dance' and signalled a great meeting of alternative-culture minds: the reigning punks meet the king of the poets.

'Inoculated City' **

Another song which sees war from the viewpoint of fallen soldiers, regardless of which side they are: "At every stroke of the bell in the tower there goes / Another boy from another side." Again downbeat, tempered, and atmospheric, it sounds more like a freeform jam with lyrics shoehorned in as an afterthought. Decent, but not memorable.

'Death is a Star' **

The closer of a refined album that was regarded as a return to form, this Jones-sung tune is laid-back and jazzy, four punks turning their hand to lounge music. Unremarkable.

Combat Rock was originally intended to be a double album, with the working title Rat Patrol From Fort Bragg. Perhaps past experience had taught the band that sometimes less is more and a number of songs were subsequently scrapped. The album's **original version** was, however, later bootlegged. The **tracklisting** for this earlier version was: 'The Beautiful People Are Ugly Too' / 'Kill Time' / 'Should I Stay Or Should I Go' / 'Rock the Casbah' / 'Know Your Rights' / 'Red Angel Dragnet' / 'Ghetto Defendant' / 'Sean Flynn' / 'Car Jamming' / 'Inoculated City' / 'Death is a Star' / 'Walk Evil Talk' / 'Atom Tan' / 'Overpowered By Funk' (demo) / 'Inoculated City' (uncensored version) / 'First Night Back In London' / 'Cool Confusion' / 'Straight to Hell' (extended mix)

CUT THE CRAP (November 4, 1985)

'Dictator' / 'Dirty Punk' / 'We Are the Clash' / 'Are You Red ...Y' / 'Cool Under Heat' / 'Movers and Shakers' / 'This Is England' / 'Three Card Trick' / 'Play to Win' / 'Fingerpoppin'' / 'North and South' / 'Life is Wild'

'Dictator' **

The Clash of 1985 bears little resemblance to the band of less than a decade earlier, and their poor final album opens with a fittingly below-par song. With Jones and Headon - arguably those with the most natural musical talent - no longer in the band, this dance track, complete with programmed drum beats and weak synthesizer horns, sounds far too much like a gimmick.

'Dirty Punk' **

A scuzzy-sounding, gutter-punk song that suffers from being both too obvious and sub-standard production; simply put, listeners can't make out what Strummer is singing. Though there is a certain anthemic quality to the chorus, it sounds like a band pretending to be The Clash rather than the band itself.

'We Are the Clash' **

A case could probably be made against 'We Are the Clash' for breaking the trade descriptions act. Critics lambasted the band for being a shadow of past glories and that much is evident on this football-terrace-style singalong. Perhaps the problem lay in so much talk of credibility and integrity in previous years; this new version of the band just couldn't compete.

'Are You Red...Y **

Though powered along by a driving machine-lead beat and a wall of power chords, 'Are You Red...Y' is interspersed with more cringeworthy and occasionally camp keyboard sounds, a weaker version of the path being taken by Mick Jones's then-emerging Big Audio Dynamite project. To be charitable, it's standard mid-80s pop. To be uncharitable, it's plain awful.

'Cool Under Heat' **

Another football-terrace chant with a hooligan stomp backbeat. Not a bad song, but with session musicians playing all the parts, 'Cool Under Heat' sounds much like a third-rate, yobby Brit-punk band, rather than the work of originators.

'Movers And Shakers' *

Again, this another song that goes nowhere, although it at least has the grace to go there quickly. Rather than building a powerful wall of sound, the use of multi-tracked vocals washes out the personality of Strummer's voice, the end result being somewhere between Oi! and synth pop, surely a combination that no one should be subjected to.

'This Is England' ***

This stand-out track, on an album later disowned by its creators, redeems things slightly. A tempered, mid-tempo song about Thatcher's decrepit and unwelcoming England, for once the keyboards and drum machine create a suitable atmosphere as Strummer sings of a place where icy winds blow and violence is dished out on the street. Not pretty, but effective. Acclaimed UK director Shane Meadows borrowed the song title for his recent excellent Thatcher-era film.

'Three Card Trick' ***

A rare rocksteady ska-reggae outing on an otherwise soulless synthetic collection, this song provides another, and possibly last, highlight on Cut The Crap. It's still nowhere near as authentic as their many fine reggae moments, though.

'Play To Win' *

A montage of street sounds and a spoken word intro from Strummer gives way to a cheaply-produced funk-pop-rock melange. A song without a centre, it has little to offer and the lyrics are borderline gibberish.

'Fingerpoppin'' *

With some heavy slap-funk bass and drums that sound like dust bin lids, 'Fingerpoppin'' is a poor stab at pop music, as generic as any chart song of the time. For a band with the pedigree of the Clash, it is little short of shameful.

'North And South' **

One of the major themes of this album is the state of Britain, and 'North And South' at least makes a few righteous punk statements about unemployment in the 80s: "It's gonna be a burn out/All around this town/The South is up/But the North is down". The anthemic quality of the music, however, brings to mind a cut-price Bruce Springsteen.

'Life Is Wild' *

And on it goes - more musical disappointments, more empty-sounding terrace chants and more crimes against an otherwise wonderful legacy. Life may be wild, but this song is just tame. What a drab end to a drab album.

COMPiLATiON/LIVE ALBUMS/BOX SETS

BLACK MARKET CLASH (1980)

B-sides and compilation tracks

'Capital Radio One' / 'The Prisoner' / 'Pressure Drop' / 'Cheat' / 'The City of the Dead' / 'Time is Tight' / 'Bankrobber/Robber Dub' / 'Armageddon Time' / 'Justice Tonight/Kick It Over'

THE STORY OF THE CLASH, VOLUME 1 (1988)

'The Magnificent Clash' / 'Rock The Casbah' / 'This Is Radio Clash' / 'Should I Stay Or Should I Go' / 'Straight to Hell' / 'Armageddon Time' / 'Clampdown' / 'Train in Vain' / 'The Guns of Brixton' / 'I Fought the Law' / 'Somebody Got Murdered' / 'Lost in the Supermarket' / 'Bank Robber' / '(White Man) In Hammersmith Palais' / 'London's Burning' / 'Janie Jones' / 'Tommy Gun' / 'Complete Control' / 'Capital Radio' / 'White Riot' / 'Career Opportunities' / 'Clash City Rockers' / 'Safe European Home' / 'Stay Free' / 'London Calling' / 'Spanish Bombs' / 'English Civil War' / 'Police & Thieves'

CLASH ON BROADWAY (November 19, 1991)

DISC 1: 'Janie Jones (demo version)' / 'Career Opportunities (demo version)' / 'White Riot' / '1977' / 'I'm So Bored With the USA' / 'Hate & War' / 'What's My Name' / 'Deny' / 'London's Burning' / 'Protex Blue' / 'Police & Thieves' / '48 Hours' / 'Cheat' / 'Garageland' / 'Capital Radio One' / 'Complete Control' / 'Clash City Rockers' / 'City of the Dead' / 'Jail Guitar Doors' / 'The Prisoner' / '(White Man) In Hammersmith Palais' / 'Pressure Drop' / '1-2 Crush on You' / 'English Civil War' (live) / 'I Fought the Law' (live)

DISC 2: 'Safe European Home' / 'Tommy Gun' / 'Julie's Been Working for the Drug Squad' / 'Stay Free' / 'One Emotion' / 'Groovy Times' / 'Gates of the West' / 'Armagideon Time' / 'London Calling' / 'Brand New Cadillac' / 'Rudie Can't Fail' / 'The Guns of Brixton' / 'Spanish Bombs' / 'Lost in the Supermarket' / 'The Right Profile' / 'The Card Cheat' / 'Death or Glory' / 'Clampdown' / 'Train in Vain' / 'Bankrobber'

DISC 3: 'Police on My Back' / 'The Magnificent Seven' / 'The Leader' / 'The Call Up' / 'Somebody Got Murdered' / 'Washington Bullets' / 'Broadway' / 'Lightning Strikes (Not Once But Twice)' / 'Every Little Bit Hurts' / 'Stop the World' / 'Midnight To Stevens' / 'This is Radio Clash' / 'Cool Confusion' / 'Red Angel

Dragnet` / 'Ghetto Defendant` / 'Rock the Casbah` / 'Should I Stay Or Should I Go` / 'Straight to Hell` / 'The Street Parade` (unlisted hidden track)

All the usual singles hits and live favourites are on this comprehensive 3-CD collection. It also includes, on Disc Three, two previously unreleased songs: the unnervingly middle-of-the-road Mick Jones-led piano ballad 'Every Little Bit Hurts`, and the low-key, affectionate tribute to producer Guy Stevens, 'Midnight To Stevens`. It also includes an unlisted track, 'The Street Parade`.

THE SINGLES (1991)

'White Riot` / 'Remote Control` / 'Complete Control` / 'Clash City Rockers` / '(White Man) In Hammersmith Palais` / 'Tommy Gun` / 'English Civil War` / 'I Fought the Law` / 'London Calling` / 'Train in Vain` / 'Bankrobber` / 'The Call Up` / 'Hitsville UK` / 'The Magnificent Seven` / 'This Is Radio Clash` / 'Know Your Rights` / 'Rock the Casbah` / 'Should I Stay Or Should I Go`

SUPER BLACK MARKET CLASH (1994)

'1977` / 'Listen` / 'Jail Guitar Doors` / 'City of the Dead` / 'The Prisoner` / 'Pressure Drop` / '1-2 Crush on You` / 'Groovy Times` / 'Gates of the West` / 'Capital Radio Two` / 'Time Is Tight` / 'Justice Tonight/Kick It Over` / 'Robber Dub` / 'The Cool Out` / 'Stop the World` / 'The Magnificent Dance` / 'Radio Clash` / 'First Night Back in London` / 'Long Time Jerk` / 'Cool Confusion`

A 1994 update of the original 10-inch-vinyl US-only 1980 release of Black Market Clash.

FROM HERE TO ETERNITY LIVE (1999)

'Complete Control` / 'London's Burning` / 'What's My Name` / 'Clash City Rockers` / 'Career Opportunities` / '(White Man) In Hammersmith Palais` / 'Capital Radio` / 'City of the Dead` / 'I Fought the Law` / 'London Calling` / 'Armagideon Time` / 'Train in Vain` / 'The Guns of Brixton` / 'The Magnificent Seven` / 'Know Your Rights` / 'Should I Stay Or Should I Go` / 'Straight to Hell`

Capturing the band at this best, **From Here To Eternity** ranks as one of the **great live albums** of recent times. The songs were recorded at variety of venues in New York and London and one in Boston between 1978 and 1982.

THE ESSENTIAL CLASH (2003)

DISC 1: 'White Riot' / '1977' / 'London's Burning' / 'Complete Control' / 'Clash City Rockers' / 'I'm So Bored With the USA' / 'Career Opportunities' / 'Hate & War' / 'Cheat' / 'Police & Thieves' / 'Janie Jones' / 'Garageland' / 'Capital Radio One' / '(White Man) In Hammersmith Palais' / 'English Civil War' / 'Tommy Gun' / 'Safe European Home' / 'Julie's Been Working For the Drug Squad' / 'Stay Free' / 'Groovy Times' / 'I Fought the Law'

DISC 2: 'London Calling' / 'The Guns of Brixton' / 'Clampdown' / 'Rudie Can't Fail' / 'Lost in the Supermarket' / 'Jimmy Jazz' / 'Train in Vain' / 'Bankrobber' / 'The Magnificent Seven' / 'Ivan Meets GI Joe' / 'Police on My Back' / 'Stop the World' / 'Somebody Got Murdered' / 'The Street Parade' / 'This Is Radio Clash' / 'Ghetto Defendant' / 'Rock the Casbah' / 'Straight to Hell' / 'Should I Stay Or Should I Go' / 'This Is England'

LONDON CALLING:
25TH ANNIVERSARY LEGACY EDITION (2004)

DISC 1: 'London Calling' / 'Brand New Cadillac' / 'Jimmy Jazz' / 'Hateful' / 'Rudie Can't Fail' / 'Spanish Bombs' / 'The Right Profile' / 'Lost in the Supermarket' / 'Clampdown' / 'The Guns of Brixton' / 'Wrong 'Em Boyo' / 'Death or Glory' / 'Koka Kola' / 'The Card Cheat' / 'Lover's Rock' / 'Four Horsemen' / 'I'm Not Down' / 'Revolution Rock' / 'Train in Vain'

DISC 2: The Vanilla Tapes: 'Hateful' / 'Rudie Can't Fail' / 'Paul's Tune' / 'I'm Not Down' / '4 Horsemen' / 'Koka Kola, Advertising & Cocaine' / 'Death or Glory' / 'Lover's Rock' / 'Lonesome Me' / 'The Police Walked In 4 Jazz' / 'Lost in the Supermarket' / 'Up-Toon' (Inst) / 'Walking the Sidewalk' / 'Where You Go Gonna Go (Soweto)' / 'The Man In Me' / 'Remote Control' / 'Working and Waiting' / 'Heart & Mind' / 'Brand New Cadillac' / 'London Calling' / 'Revolution Rock'

This 25th anniversary release came with a second disc entitled The Vanilla Tapes, featuring 'London Calling'-era studio jams, instrumentals, and demos, recently unearthed at home by Mick Jones. Because these songs were never intended for release it would be unfair to grade them alongside their released work. Though rudimentary, The Vanilla Tapes do, however, provide a worthwhile insight into the development of the album as the band branched out into other styles and cover versions (Bob Dylan's 'The Man In Me', Vince Taylor's rockabilly standard 'Brand New Cadillac), and the productivity of a band at a creative peak. Some songs feature working titles, such as 'Paul's Tune', later reworked and recorded as 'The

Guns of Brixton'. It's definitely worth investigating to hear the bare bones of the album London Calling.

SINGLES BOX (2006)

DISC 1: 'White Riot' / '1977'

DISC 2: 'Listen' (edit / 'Interview On the Circle Line', by Tony Parsons) / 'Interview On the Circle Line Part II' / 'Capital Radio One'

DISC 3: 'Remote Control' / 'London's Burning' (Live) / 'London's Burning'

DISC 4: 'Complete Control' / 'City of the Dead'

DISC 5: 'Clash City Rockers' / 'Jail Guitar Doors'

DISC 6: '(White Man) In Hammersmith Palais' / 'The Prisoner'

DISC 7: 'Tommy Gun' / '1-2 Crush On You'

DISC 8: 'English Civil War' / 'Pressure Drop'

DISC 9: 'I Fought the Law' / 'Groovy Times' / 'Gates of the West' / 'Capital Radio Two'

DISC 10: 'London Calling' / 'Armagideon Time' / 'Justice Tonight' / 'Kick It Over' / 'Clampdown' / 'The Card Cheat' / 'Lost in the Supermarket'

DISC 11: 'Bankrobber' / 'Rockers Galore ... UK Tour' (Feat. Mikey Dread) / 'Rudie Can't Fail' / 'Train in Vain'

DISC 12: 'The Call Up' / 'Stop the World'

DISC 13: 'Hitsville UK' / 'Radio One' / 'Police on My Back' / 'Somebody Got Murdered'

DISC 14: 'The Magnificent Seven' (Edit) / 'The Magnificent Seven' (Edit) / 'Lightning Strikes (Not Once But Twice)' / 'One More Time' / 'One More Dub' / 'The Cool Out' / 'The Magnificent Seven' (twelve inch version) / 'The Magnificent Dance' (12 twelve inch version)

DISC 15: 'This Is Radio Clash' / 'Radio Clash' / 'Outside Broadcast' / 'Radio 5'

DISC 16: 'Know Your Rights' / 'First Night Back in London'

DISC 17: 'Rock the Casbah' / 'Long Time Jerk' / 'Mustapha Dance' / 'Red Angel Dragnet' / 'Overpowered by Funk'

DISC 18: 'Should I Stay Or Should I Go' / 'Straight to Hell' (Edited Version) / 'Inoculated City' / 'Cool Confusion'

DISC 19: 'This Is England' / 'Do It Now' / 'Sex Mad Roar'

The Clash's complete singles and EP discography, released as a CD singles box set and including various bonus tracks and alternative versions, such as instrumentals and original 12-inch mixes. Great songs, great packaging, and sleeve notes from a number of celebrity fans - though one does wonder how many more versions of The Clash's discography the record label will manage to squeeze out.

UK SiNGLES DiSCOGRAPHY

The content of these songs are explored above, but for reference, here is The Clash's UK seven and 12-inch singles discography with full tracklistings.

'White Riot' / '1977' (March 18 1977)

'Capital Radio' / 'Interview' / 'Listen' (Free EP given away to NME readers, April 9, 1977)

'Remote Control' / 'London's Burning' (May 13 1977)

'Complete Control' / 'City Of the Dead' (September 23 1977)

'Clash City Rockers' / 'Jail Guitar Doors' (February 17 1978)

'White Man (In Hammersmith Palais)' / 'The Prisoner' (June 16 1978)

'Tommy Gun' / '1-2 Crush On You' (November 24 1978)

'English Civil War' / 'Pressure Drop' (February 23 1979)

The Cost of Living EP ('I Fought the Law' / 'Groovy Times' / 'Gates of the West' / 'Capital Radio' (May 11 1979)

'London Calling' / 'Armagideon Time' (December 7 1979)

'London Calling' / 'Armagideon Time' / 'Justice Tonight' / 'Kick It Over' (12", January 4 1980)

'Bankrobber' / 'Rockers Galore' (August 8 1980)

'The Call Up' / 'Stop the World' (November 21 1980)

'Hitsville UK' / 'Radio One' (January 16 1981)

'The Magnificent Seven' / 'Magnificent Dance' (7" and 12", April 10 1981)

'This Is Radio Clash' / 'Radio Clash' (November 20, 1981)

'This Is Radio Clash' / 'Radio Clash' / 'Outside Broadcast' / 'Radio 5' (12", November 20, 1981)

'Know Your Rights' / 'First Night Back in London' (April 23 1982)

'Rock the Casbah' / 'Long Time Jerk' (7" and 7" picture disc June 11 1982)

'Rock the Casbah' / 'Mustapha Dance' (12", June 11 1982)

'Should I Stay Or Should I Go' / 'Straight to Hell' (7", 7" picture disc and 12", September 17 1982)

'This Is England' / 'Do It Now' (September 30 1985)

'This Is England' / 'Do It Now' / 'Sex Mad War' (September 30 1985)

Most of **The Clash's singles** have been re-issued, featuring previously released material as B-sides, both during the band's career and afterwards - most notably the chart-topping Levi's advert tie-in release of 'Should I Stay Or Should I Go' in 1991.